## LETS GO United States of America!

# It's Time for the
# John Doe Party!

### We can no longer count on Republicans for heavy lifting.

On Mayday, 2017, the Republican Party showed that the will of regular people in the Party matters not an iota. Republican elite leadership once again turned over the control of the budget to the Democrats. Hard as it is to believe, the truth is more difficult to assimilate than the fake news.

Ant-leftists, conservatives, nationalists, populists and regular Americans for America, who might very well be described simply as Trump voters and loyalists, learned a bitter lesson again watching Republican Party leaders give it up for the opposition party. We need a representative party that we can count on. That representation has not been delivered by the weak-kneed, elitist establishment Republican leadership. In the first budget submission of the Trump Administration, they found our backs and stabbed us again.

This book describes the values that are no longer important to Republicans and it offers a John Doe American solution so that the one-time Party of Lincoln is no longer important to everyday John Does. This book delivers a comprehensive rationale for why the Republican Party must be abandoned in favor of a brand new American Party that we would do well with the name The John Doe Party. The John Doe Party will soon be the rallying party for all the nobodies in America who love America. Gary Cooper and Frank Capra would call us all "John Does." The John Doe Party needs to replace the Republican Party. We do not need a Party that cannot be trusted?

Americans believed we threw out the swamp with Donald Trump's election yet, the elite establishment Republicans did not get the message. For example, anybody working on an Omnibus solution regarding the 2017 budget would have designed it to help build a better America. Republicans unfortunately are way too happy with Obamacare light, the baby killing Planned Parenthood, living without a secure Southern Wall, and the many other dictates imposed from donors and Republican Party elites who cannot understand the people's trust in President Trump.

The John Doe Party is the best choice for regular Americans.

**LETS
GO
PUBLISH**

# BRIAN W. KELLY

**Published by**:            LETS GO PUBLISH!
**Publisher & Editor:**      Brian P. Kelly
**Email:**                   info@letsgopublish.com
                             www.letsgopublish.com


Library of Congress Copyright Information Pending
**Book Cover Design by Brian W. Kelly;  Editing by Brian P. Kelly**

**ISBN Information:** The International Standard Book Number (ISBN) is a unique machine-readable identification number, which marks any book unmistakably. The ISBN is the clear standard in the book industry. 159 countries and territories are officially ISBN members. The Official ISBN For this book is **978-0-9988111-7-8**

---

The price for this work is :                                    **$9.95 USD**

10      9      8      7      6      5      4      3      2      1

Release Date:                                                    June 2017

LETS
GO
PUBLISH!

# Dedication

*I dedicate this book*

*To my wonderful children—Brian, Mike, and Katie, and their wonderful mother, Patricia.*

*We are a close family and my children help in every way they can to assure the muse is always fired up.*

*Thank you all!*

# Acknowledgments

In every book that I write or edit, I publicly acknowledged all the help that I have received from many sources. Some of these wonderful people are still living on earth and others have made their way to heaven.

I would like to thank many people for helping me in this effort.

I have listed their names and the story I usually tell on the Lets Go Publish! Web site-- www.letsgopublish.com. Look for the main menu on the left side of the site. Please take a run out there and you will find the text about all of those who are acknowledged for their help in bringing my books to you.

God bless you all for your help.

My plan is to make necessary changes to the acknowledgments on the LGP web site as often as I can so that I can update the status of the many who for so long helped me with my books.

Thank you all for all your help in keeping Lets Go Publish and the folks at Amazon, (www.amazon.com/author/brianwkelly) on the top of the heap for so long.

Thank you all on the big list in the sky.

In this book, I received some extra special help from many friends including Dennis Grimes, Gerry Rodski, Wily Ky Eyely, Angel Irene McKeown Kelly, Angel Edward Joseph Kelly Sr., Angel Edward Joseph Kelly Jr., Ann Flannery, Angel James Flannery Sr., Mary Daniels, Bill Daniels, Robert Garry Daniels, Angel Sarah Janice Daniels, Angel Punkie Daniels, Angels Brady and Ben Kelly, Joe Kelly and Diane Kelly.

To sum up my acknowledgments, as I do in every book that I have written, I am compelled to offer that I am truly convinced that "the only thing one can do alone in life is fail." Thanks to my family, good friends, and a wonderful helping team, I am not alone.


Thank you all

Brian W. Kelly

# Table of Contents

(

# Table of Contents

# Preface:

Republicans were AWOL during the Obama presidency, and we quickly learned when they submitted their Mayday Budget in 2017 that the Party plan is to remain AWOL.

Once thought to be honest to a fault, the Republicans have taken to lying as a tool to survive. However, as neophytes in the lying game, they are not as good as Democrats, and they do not have the corrupt press available to back up everything they say.

Republicans chose a while ago to no longer care about the needs of any in the Republican Party other than the fat-cat donors and the K-street lobbyists, and the Party elites. They blamed conservatives for losing the Presidency in 2012, yet it was the Republican Party who backed an elite Republican not the anti-leftist conservatives, nationalists, populists, or regular Americans.

Though Mitt Romney was not a bad guy in 2012, and he may have made an OK president, he was not a good candidate for regular Americans, and he did not attract the masses of John Does to the Republican Party.

It really does not matter at this point as it is almost a certainty that Republicans for some time now have been looking for a new constituent base. Anti-leftist, non-elites without huge checkbook balances to the Republican Party today are passé. Wildly dreaming Republicans were hoping that Hispanics would become their new base, and Paul Ryan was commissioned to roll regular John Does off a cliff along with Granny.

While Republicans planned the demise of the little guys in the party, Americans who love America decided to launch a preemptive strike on the elite Republican establishment. We looked for and found a candidate that the wimpy, RINO, establishment Republicans did not want. That man of course is Donald Trump. He is now our President. His election shows that the people can do anything when motivated.

This book asks regular Americans such as anti-leftists, conservatives, nationalists, populists, independents, and regular American John Does who love America to strongly consider pulling out of the Republican

Party. They have left us behind and they are not looking back to see if we are following. Even regular John Doe Democrats will be welcomed in The John Doe Party.

The good ole boy elite establishment Republicans can learn to swim in their own complacency. America-lovers, conservatives and former Tea Party people, who most often are one and the same, for eight years had a real enemy in the White House. His name as we well know is Barack Hussein Obama, and he had appointed his heir to be Hillary Rodham Clinton. Of course, we the people did not want that and we made Donald Trump President of all America.

Why is this book about Republican leadership instead of the Democratic leadership? Democrats are always the clear and present danger to democracy. The answer hit me like a ton of bricks. It was a wake-up call. What seemed like out of nowhere, the GOP began to stop engaging Democrats as an opposition party by choosing not to help regular Americans fight the many Obama anti-American policies. Worse than that, with Trump's ascendancy to the presidency, the Republican RINOs continued to favor Democrats over the anti-leftists John Does that had always supported the Party of Lincoln.

It seemed like a bad dream when Republicans began to either believe they were dealt a winning hand in the Obama game or they were actually afraid of the President. Either way, these were scary times for Americans. No reinforcements came to the aid of Americans from the Republican Party, who had simply capitulated. Regular Americans now must get accustomed to getting nothing from Republicans. We must be prepared to go it alone. When Donald Trump showed up, we knew we had our leader; now we must fight to gain real representation.

For years, Americans believed that the Republican Party's values and our values were the same. Regular Americans have not had our own Party, and so for many years or so it seemed, Republicans were the enforcers for our values. Therefore, we logically believed that Republicans felt the same about important matters as we do. We were wrong. Republicans idiotically made their love affairs with the donor class and the K-street lobbyists well known and began to oppose regular Americans in important life and values matters.

In the Economy and in foreign affairs, Obama spent eight years in an anti-American role. During this time. The Republican leadership has been marking time choosing not to oppose the Democrats. Republicans became the great pretenders bluffing us that "our day would come," without any pushback to the Obama agenda.

That's why this book and The John Doe Party are so necessary today. We unabashedly recommend that Americans stop trusting Republican hand-shakers. They have proven that they will not fight for America or for American values. Their own greed trumps the needs of America. The leaders of the Grand Old Party have not even acknowledged that Obama and the Democrats are wrong. Anti-leftist regular Americans such as you and I must learn to go it along.

The sooner Americans can cast off Republicans as our only protection against Democrats and progressivism, the sooner we can move on to solving the problem for our values, our country, and our freedom. We need our own Party for sure; for without a Party, Regular John Doe Americans will not even be permitted to help on the battlefield when America is hanging by just a thread.

While we have been waiting for the right time to form a party, most of us think that we can defeat the Democrat leadership, the corporations, the unions, the media, and the traitorous Republicans who are not worth the ground they stand on. The time for waiting is over. It is now time to act.

As a great start, Americans from all political backgrounds chose to support Trump as our President. What a great move. He will govern as a good Republican, unless he too gets frustrated with the anti-Trump power brokers in the GOP and must rally the troops such as us, without the Republican Party umbrella. We must stand ready to do our part within a new Party—The John Doe Party.

We must work together to form The John Doe Party of John Doe Americans—the little guys in America, and leave the elite establishment to run its own party. Meanwhile, The John Doe Party takes all the regulars in America, including the regular Joe Democrats, Independents and members of other parties who love America. We can do it. Our first step was to get Trump elected and we did that. We the people can do anything. Now that we are motivated, it is time to move forward.

Brian W. Kelly for years and years has monitored what is happening to regular Americans and has written extensively on this major problem with the Republican Party. He is one of America's most outspoken and eloquent conservative on American values. He is the author of 116 books including Saving America The Trump Way, Why Trump? Taxation without Representation, Obama's Seven Deadly Sins, Kill the EPA! Jobs! Jobs! Jobs! and many other fine patriotic books.

All Kelly books are now available at Amazon, and Kindle. Many can be found at Barnes & Noble and other fine booksellers. www.amazon.com/author/brianwkelly. Like most of you, Brian is fed up with a stifling progressive liberal agenda in Washington that places the needs of everybody else in front of the needs of Americans who love America. Like many regular John Does, he is shocked at the behavior of the new RINO Republican Party.

Like you, Kelly is frustrated at how Republicans continually try to deceive us so that we will believe they are still with US on values and policy. They want our votes but they no longer want to know what we think. It does not matter to these establishment elites.

Brian Kelly has read the intelligence reports, has researched and has written about these important topics for years, and he knows how intolerable the results of poor government policy can be within our neighborhoods. His comprehensible and sane recommendations in this book are explained in detail within the covers of this soon-to-be classic offering.

More and more Americans are clamoring for jobs but all that has been given by the prior President and his coterie was lip service. Republicans permitted it and are ready to fight President Donald Trump to assure there is no improvement. We cannot let this stand. Americans wanted to keep their health insurance and pick their own doctors. Yet, Republicans, who can help change this for Americans have decided to cave to Democrats. Why was there no repeal of Obamacare?

Obama was a fine politician and he continues to make his case for his legacy. We cannot afford to be fooled again even if Republican leaders choose to continue sucking up to the Obama Shadow Government. Unbelievable as it may seem, Republicans have decided to give him what he wants by giving his legacy all the money they need to continue his agenda. The John Doe Party, when elected ASAP will end this practice.

*It's Time for the John Doe Party!* Is the bible to get us back on track with America. It shows why sucking up to RINO Republicans is bad for Americans, and Kelly tells us all what to do about it. You are going to love this book since it is designed by an American for Americans. Few books are a must-read but *It's Time for the John Doe Party!* has the prospects of ending the party of elites paid for by the US taxpayers.

Thanks to you, *It's Time for the John Doe Party!* is about to appear at the top of America's most read list.

Sincerely,

Brian P. Kelly, Editor

# About the Author

Brian W. Kelly retired as an Assistant Professor in the Business Information Technology (BIT) program at Marywood University, where he also served as the IBM i and midrange systems technical advisor to the IT faculty. Kelly designed, developed, and taught many college and professional courses. He is also a contributing technical editor to a number of IT industry magazines, including "The Four Hundred" and "Four Hundred Guru" published by IT Jungle.

Kelly is a former IBM Senior Systems Engineer and he has been a candidate for US Congress and the US Senate from Pennsylvania. He has an active information technology consultancy. He is the author of 116 books and numerous articles about current IT issues and general topics. For years, was a frequent speaker at COMMON, IBM conferences, and other technical conferences, & user group meetings across the US. Ask him to talk at your next John Doe Club meeting!

Over the past eight years, Brian Kelly has become one of America's most outspoken and eloquent conservative protagonists. Besides this book, Kelly has also written *Taxation Without Representation*, *Obama's Seven Deadly Sins*, *Healthcare Accountability*, *Kill the EPA*, *Jobs! Jobs! Jobs!*, *Saving America*, *RRR*, *Why Trump?*, and many other books designed to help America and Americans.

Endorsed by the Independence Hall Tea Party in 2010, Kelly ran for Congress against a 13-term Democrat and, took no campaign contributions, spent enough to buy signs and T-shirts, and as a virtual unknown, he captured 17% of the vote— www.briankellyforcongress.com.

# Chapter 1 What's Wrong with Republicans?

## Regular Americans are mad as hell

Anti-left John Doe style regular Americans who once considered themselves pure bread conservatives are not alone in being upset today with many things, including a corrupt Congress, and an inept government. People of many political persuasions came out of the woodwork in late 2016 to express their outrage by voting for Donald Trump for President.

For eight years, the prior President, BHO, unlawfully bypassed the Constitution to do whatever he wanted to the country. Meanwhile wimpy Republicans in positions of power did not eve complain and actually appeared to be going along to get along. That made the John Does such as yours truly "Mad as Hell!"

Howard Beale in the paragraphs below represents all frustrated Americans. His story, though unrelated, really captures the mood and the emotions of America today regarding a government and a Republican Party gone bad!

You may not remember because you are probably not old enough but many others of you have enough years to have seen the movie long after its debut in 1976. So, if you have some baggage, and you have some time on your bones, you may remember back in November 1976 when Howard Beale, as played by Peter Finch, the long-time anchor in the movie "Network News," gets the bad news that eventually causes him to utter one of the most famous movie lines of all time.

Beale gets fired and is given two weeks. The long-time anchor has a very poor reaction to this news and he cannot control himself during the next news broadcast.

He promises to commit suicide on the air. The company immediately fires him—no second chances for a repeat performance. Beale is devastated and remorseful. He begs for the opportunity to say good-by to his fans with dignity, and he is reluctantly given his last opportunity ever for air time so that he can say his good-by's and also apologize. He gets his chance

Yet, once on the air, Beale is overwhelmed by his continuing circumstance. He goes into another diatribe starting off with a rant claiming that "Life is bullshit." He is so passionate that his ratings spike as he persuades his viewers to shout out of their windows: "I'm as mad as hell, and I'm not going to take this anymore!" That is the line heard 'round the world.

Well, my fellow Americans, I bet you saw this coming, and I am going to deliver it as passionately in words as I can: "I am mad as hell, and I am not going to take this anymore." I bet you are too. Let me remind you.

Taxes are too high; elected officials are out of touch; government is too big; spending is out of control; the Affordable Healthcare has become a train wreck; heroes are dying in the VA system, and nobody, after spending $160 billion per year supposedly on Veterans, can tell us why they are being neglected.

The people of America see the federal government for the last eight years as incompetent. We elected Republicans to have a voice, and yet we have no voice as they do what helps them and their elite donors, not us. Americans have no voice. We exchanged five top Taliban Officers from Gitmo for one deserter PFC. Additionally, and this is the worst: too many of US are too lazy to hold government accountable, and too many of our finest are on the take from elite donors and from insiders on K-Street.

It really is a train wreck. Corporate leaches have infiltrated our government and they seem to have a grip on Republican lawmakers. We have record unemployment; illegal aliens are smiling as they take American jobs; an unsustainable status quo supports special interests over the people's interests and when we look to the future we see a public education system that creates dummies and it trains k to 12 and college students to love the government. The graduates are so dumb that they don't seem to mind being called dummies. Scrooge would sum it up with a hearty "Bah Humbug." It is that bad!

We have had the poorest economy since the depression; excessive welfare; income and healthcare redistribution; institutionalized lying; a corrupt state-loving press carrying water for government; a debt large enough to kill America; huge student debt stopping graduates' successes; tyranny v. democracy; government lawlessness; support for criminals over police; freedom and liberty in jeopardy; American stagnation, and a big loss of America's world prestige.

And, on top of that, the press beats its breast about its importance by suggesting that the former president learned about what was happening across the world from reading the newspapers. Meanwhile government is spying on the people—even the newly elected president. Everybody in Washington gets a free ride with no accountability. It is that bad.

Our big government has become such a problem that most Americans believe that it can never again be the solution. Republicans choose to behave like Democrats rather than take them on. Our finest hope, our youth; go through colleges in huge numbers only to be unemployed and sacked with debt for life. As a Democrat, I am smarter than most. I know that the Democratic Party is the source of most ill fortune in the country. But, millennials do not believe it so they are not willing to fight the bad guys in either party to make America great again!

This group of youngins known as millennials are the smartest by cranium but they are the stupidest offspring America has ever produced from anybody's loins in terms of their gullibility and their willingness to sacrifice their future for a promising promise.

They have no clue what life is about and they actually protest American heroes such as Condoleezza Rice and Dr. Ben Carson. Both came to visit universities and were disrespected by the students. Rutgers for example in 2013 picked a boardwalk babe, Snooki, rather than an American who loves America to give them their final addresses at their Universities. Even Berkley will not permit free speech anymore and will not protect those who insist on it. The have small free speech zones on many college campuses so that free speech does not get in the way of their preferred propaganda. Hope is reserved for people who have never met today's millennials.

Students are guided by coffee-breath communist professors in universities and the students now accept that communism is OK. These are the elite progressives in their universities who believe free speech cannot be tolerated and who fill the heads of the millennials with mush. Their importance is endorsed by the universities when they get to be adorned in their finest plumage at commencement ceremonies, and they process before all others to the stage. With such guidance, students have learned that they really do know it all, though their parents have no clue what happens to them once they reach progressive campuses.

The student loan burden prevents former student borrowers from buying homes, cars, and having a family. Yet students do not blame their elite faculty and their establishment universities for anything. They blame George Bush for everything still because some talk show host once told them that works for him. They have begun to blame President Trump but gave Obama a free pass. It is great to have brains today, it is just not respected if one decides to use them for the public good.

Only retirees in their 90's can afford honeymoon cottages while looking for their next spouse. As many as 37 million student loan borrowers are too broke to engage in basic life. College loans, instead of lifting people to the top, have created a new race to the bottom,

On the International stage, America is a bad actor, and frustrated zealots from the left are making sure nobody gives America a break on the world stage. For eight years, the US tried to make the rest of the world strong by making America weak. The weaknesses of America are highlighted by a corrupt press because Americans have been doing too well and their perspective because of a new phenomenon known as "white privilege."

None of this helps command respect for our country from anybody but the guilt-ridden university students and their "lucky to have a job" mentors on the faculty. Having been a faculty member, I know how bad things are. The only people who seem to care have names like John Q. Public, John Doe, and Jane Doe. Thank you to the Johns and the Janes for choosing this book about a solution to the country's mess.

Nobody in the world gives America standing ovations anymore. Nobody asks us for curtain calls. Our leaders for eight years turned their backs on our friends and paid homage to our enemies. How is this? We now have a President who was elected to drain the swamp but the Republican Congress seem to like living in the Swamp and they resist the President's overtures to make America great again.

Has Congress lost all its power? Or has Congress decided to simply give up. Who has the power in the US? The Constitution says it is the people! We replaced the President in 2016 and we must do the same for the Congress in 2018. If the Congress won't help the President drain the swamp, Congress should be taken out of their self-created swamp and sent back to live in an ungated community.

Before Donald Trump bombed the Syrian Airport and let the MOAB fly down on the caves, smaller and weaker countries such as Russia, Iran, and North Korea continued to push the US around and laugh at US, and our only response was to see if somehow it might have been because we may have offended them.

We once could not figure out any other way to show our greatness than by counting the number of hits on a *hashtag of **bring our girls home,*** when no Americans were missing, and we expected terrorists to cower when the number of twitter resends hits a million.

Over the last eight years, US officials refused to have an honest discussion about why four Americans, including the US Ambassador, were permitted to die in Benghazi when the military says they were prepared to save them. The then Secretary of State responsible for their deaths is then able to run for President as if their deaths did not matter. How does that happen in America? What Republican that you know spoke up about it?

We had an administration that blames the Christian Government of Nigeria for not reaching out enough to the Muslim killers who kidnapped 300 girls for sex slaves.  Boko Haram had captured and killed 49 boys just a few weeks before.

The captors boldly announced they would sell them on the sex slave market, and the US was powerless in its feeble response. The new strategy is to have time go by so those who are at fault can claim that it is old news.

What has happened to our good sense? Should there not be a set of laws written by sane people so that insane acts cannot occur without retribution? Why do our representatives, especially Republicans who have lost heart not represent America?

For me, these are the worst days of America that I have ever witnessed. Yet, our recent government seemed to have no problems that need solutions. Clear-thinking Americans look at today's Republican leaders as buffoons, without the wherewithal to tie their own shoes. We yearned for a guy like Donald Trump to come forth to save us. And yet while he is prepared to do so, Republican Never Trumpers are willing to give America the five-finger salute to express their displeasure with our very capable President. These leaders would like all Americans to be happy in a state of mediocrity, rather than being outstanding. "Don't worry: Be Happy!"

If you have been paying attention, and I sure hope you have been as it is a civic duty, you know that there are even more issues than the exhaustive list we just walked you through. Isn't that a shame on US? I think this is the reason that you bought this book. Thank you very much. The Constitution is a survivor's guide to dealing with a corrupt nation; a corrupt press; a corrupt government and corrupt politicians who believe they can trick you into finding them acceptable. Armed with the Constitution, we John Does must get rid of the Republican party and replace it with a new party for us—for the people. Yes, the

John Doe Party is the people's solution to corrupt greedy Republican elite politicians and their donor class.

Since you bought this book, I know you and I are on the right side and thankfully we are on the same side. Together, we can all help arrest control of our government back from perpetrators wishing to destroy US and a Republican Party that is determined not to lift a finger until we are destroyed from within.

We first must understand what is going on and we then must understand our rights. Even before you and me and everybody else are on board, just like Howard Beale, we must start the first wave of solutions by opening our windows all the way and shouting as loud as we all can: "I am mad as hell, and I am not going to take this anymore."

Then, we must make sure that we talk to everybody we know on the streets, supermarkets, and the neighborhoods—people like you and I and others, and let's help them all know that unless we all fully engage in America, when we wake up from our deep fog, there may be no America left for our progeny. We will have blown it for sure if that is permitted to happen.

Getting The John Doe Party off the ground is a great start.

# Chapter 2 Heritage Foundation Says Don't Be Snookered.

## Republicans still snooker the people

Republicans were once solid on doing what was right for America. Democrats always talked the better game but handed the outhouse spoon to Americans as the fulfillment of their promise. After Americans voted in Donald Trump and a Republican House and Senate with the expressed purpose of draining the swamp, Republicans chose not to make it happen. In its first noteworthy act of this Congressional session, the Republican leadership decided to protect the swamp and drain the people of any financial influence in the government. No, I am not kidding.

The Heritage Foundation supports regular Americans. They put together an analysis of the Republican charade. They wrote a great synopsis of the message sent by Republican Elites on Mayday, 2017 in the Omnibus Budget. The Republicans supported every Democrat notion that Obama had put in his budget from last year, and even some Obama had forgotten. And, they gave the Democrats 1.1 Billion spending money for whatever they wanted. But, they provided the people with no wall and they refused to begin draining the swamp. Doesn't that upset you? Doesn't that make you mad as hell. The Republicans betrayed the people.

Here is a piece written by Heritage. You will be further enraged after you digest what the Republicans just did to us

**KEY VOTE: "NO" ON FY17 OMNIBUS SPENDING BILL (H.R. 244)**

**MAY 02, 2017**

This week, the House and Senate will consider the Consolidated Appropriations Act of 2017 (H.R. 244), a 1,665-page omnibus spending package that would fund the federal government through September 30, 2017. The Heritage Foundation explains that while the bill, which was released publicly at 2 AM Monday morning, "does make progress" on some issues, "it woefully fails the test of fiscal responsibility and does not advance important conservative policies."

Many conservatives went along with a short-term continuing resolution last December based on a promise that the current deadline would be used to advance key policy priorities. Instead, the bill is widely viewed as a rebuke to President Trump's agenda and conservative priorities.

Overall, the Trump administration requested an additional $30 billion in military, $1.5 billion to continue construction of the southern border wall, and $18 billion in discretionary cuts. The bill provides only $15 billion for defense (of which $2.5 billion is withheld until the administration submits a plan to combat ISIS), provides no funding for the border wall, and actually increases domestic discretionary spending. Through a combination of emergency funding and overseas contingency operations funds, the bill pushes discretionary spending $93 billion above the budget caps.

The Trump administration was rebuked at the program level as well. The Department of Energy's Office of Science will receive an additional $42 million, whereas the administration requested a $900 million reduction. Funding for Community Development Block Grants was kept level despite a $1.5 billion requested reduction. The list goes on, as CQ Roll Call reported: "Trump proposed killing off more than a dozen federal programs in his fiscal 2018 budget outline, but it doesn't appear appropriators are inclined to reduce or eliminate federal funding for any of those line items."

Liberals celebrated the bill as a victory over President Trump and claimed they successfully blocked "more than 160 Republican poison pill riders." Heritage notes the omnibus "fails to advance almost any key conservative policies" as "it would continue to provide funding for Planned Parenthood and do nothing to restrict funding to sanctuary cities."

Along with a lack of conservative policy riders, the bill contains a $1.3 billion bailout for the United Workers of America, a union that represents about 10 percent of all coal production in the U.S. today. Coal miners deserve proper health care and retirement benefits, but it is the job of the union and private companies that made those promises, not taxpayers, to provide those benefits.

H.R. 244 contains a second health care bailout to Puerto Rico. In passing a bill to help Puerto Rico restructure its debts last year, lawmakers promised there would be no cash bailout. Yet, this bill would give the mismanaged and politically corrupt Puerto Rican government $296 million in taxpayer dollars to cover their shortage in Medicaid funds.

Coupled with these two bailouts, the omnibus spending bill also funds liberal priorities and initiatives. H.R. 244 includes millions in increased funding for Department of Energy (DOE) pet projects, national parks, Amtrak, Head Start, college tuition assistance, the National Endowments for the Arts and Humanities, the Transportation Security Administration (TSA), and even a Bureau of Land Management (BLM) sage grouse conservation project.

When spending bills provide more funding to the National Institutes of Health (NIH) than border security, as this bill does, it's fair for conservatives to ask if this resembles more of an Obama administration-era spending bill than a Trump one.

The Heritage Foundation's Justin Bogie and Rachel Greszler acknowledge the bill "does make progress" on some issues, but they add:

*"Unfortunately, the additional $15 billion in defense spending is only half of what President Donald Trump requested earlier this year and is inadequate to meet global threats facing the country.*

*"The additional $1.5 billion for border security is important in the battle to curb illegal immigration. However, none of these funds can be used for construction of a border wall, one of the president's top priorities.*

*"Unfortunately, none of the increases in spending proposed by this bill would be offset. Earlier this year, the president released a 'skinny budget' which proposed $18 billion in 2017 cuts, yet none of those cuts made it into the latest budget deal."*

**Heritage Action opposes H.R. 244 and will include it as a key vote on our legislative scorecard.**

# Chapter 3  Republicans Have Betrayed Their Voters!

## Who do you trust?

As discussed in Chapter 2, The House was wrapping up negotiations on the big Omnibus the Sunday before Mayday 2017. It was a joint effort of the Congress (House) of the United States and the President, held behind closed doors. The result was that the Republicans agreed to stiff the American people on the extension of the 2017 budget known as the Omnibus.

Americans have become accustomed to lies and even bigger lies from our elected officials but few of us expected President Trump to join the party. We hope our President is working on a special deal but right now, to a lot of regular Americans, it seems that we have been the victims of a major prevarication that was not an accident.

The official word from whitehouse.gov is as follows: "**If the Consolidated Appropriations Act, 2017 were presented to the President in its current form, his advisors would recommend that he sign the bill into law.**" We can only pray that our real President reappears, takes the Heritage Foundation's advice, and vetoes this bill. At the same time, let's hope the President of the US sends the President of the Swamp, Special Interests, and the Republican Leadership back into hiding.

We all know that there could be no budget celebration this week without President Trump going along with the partiers just to get along. It surely does not sound like the modus operandi of our formerly tough and triumphant head of state. Maybe it is just part of deal-making but many anti-leftists are very concerned.

It is killing folks like me that our President is now taking cues from swamp people—most of whom are Republican Party wimps and long-term Trump haters. What is up?

One school of thought says that the President has resigned himself into believing that he can eat crow dinners in perpetuity and his loyal constituents such as you and I, will not notice. They are dead wrong. Mr. President, we have noticed. We can see the feathers between your teeth. I am sorry to say.

None of us are happy about the new you. Bring back the old Donald J. Trump, please even though the new you is much better than Obama. Yes, we blame the Republican House Leadership first but they can't have their way without your full complicity.

What happened Mr. President to your toughness and excess mettle. Please go back into the drawer where you put your good stuff, and take it out again and start wearing it again. We still need you and we will forgive you. You are not one of them. Please do not become one of them for too long.

Democrats, of course, have claimed a huge victory that they blocked the Trump agenda. That is not good news. They are our opponents.

For the first time in years, this time, they are telling the truth. They did block the Trump agenda and substituted their own. It was a masterful trick for a bunch of losers. Their clear budget victory took the wind out of the sails of a lot of hopeful Trump loyalists.

Americans expect nothing from Democrats and so there is little anger against them. Republicans offered real American regular people hope, but they chose to fail again on purpose as they really do not want the swamp to be drained. It's tough to believe Republicans will ever get the people's wish list done. You remember that list—it was once Donald Trump's to-do-list.

The day before Mayday, campaign promises no longer mattered. This gave the Democrats their victory and that was all that mattered to lying Republicans who for years asked for one more thing and one more thing to have enough power to fight the Democrats. Now, with more than enough power, they decided to implement the Democratic agenda saying to hell with the people "what brung us."

To be sure the news was true, many Americans went back to the stories of the election day results and they learned again that the Democrats did not win. So, if they did not win, why are they able to keep beating up Republicans? Answer: Only because the Republicans want to be beaten up!

The Republicans did it all without the help of Democrats but it pleases the Democrats to no end. The Republican Party showed that the vote of the people did not matter an iota as they willingly and gleefully turned over the control of the precious US budget to the same Democrats, who had lost it all in the last election. Yes, the Democrats who blamed the Russians for their loss. Same Democrats. The people had voted but their representatives did not choose to hear the message. Hard as it is to believe, the truth is more difficult sometimes to assimilate than the fake news.

Anti-left Americans as well as nationalists, populists, and of course Americans for America, who might very well be described simply as Trump voters, swamp-drainers, and Trump loyalists learned a bitter lesson again in trusting Republicans to do the right thing. When the news eked out that the Democrats had a big budget win, it was also known that the people had a big loss because the Republicans chose to have a big budget loss. Republicans had the power and they voted to lose.

This is a story told often in the last six years of Obama times. Republicans offered one excuse after another as Obama and company were ripping apart America. Republicans tried to explain it away by saying it was necessary to get any deal. A bad deal is not a deal, it is a giveaway.

Rather than forcing the Democrats to shut down our poorly run government, cowardly Republicans chose to give them it all. Republican double dealers even gave Democrats little things that the President really wanted just to rub salt in his wounds. The Congressional leadership does not act like they like our President. Maybe we need to replace them.

The Omnibus Bill seemed to be written by the staffs of the Donor class, Lobbyists and K-street insiders to keep their coffers full and say: "to the nether world with the American people." Then the shrewd Republican Never-Trump leadership claimed a victory after giving the house away. They continue to hope the people are stupid and that we believe they really won and the Democrats lost. Not even close. The Dems scored a big one. The Republicans took a fall for their donors who like the swamp.

When you read about the bill, for you won't want to read the 1600+ pages of government-ese, in which you will specifically see how the President and the people were stiffed. For example, as noted in the brief Heritage analysis, the bill provides only $15 billion for defense (of which $2.5 billion is withheld until the administration submits a plan to combat ISIS).

The bill provides no funding for the border wall. Yes, that's right, Trump's #1 issue! He was stiffed on that too. The bill actually increases domestic discretionary spending. Through a combination of emergency funding and overseas contingency operations funds, the bill pushes discretionary spending $93 billion above the budget caps. Democrats love the spending increases. The people did not win on this one.

The Trump administration was rebuked at the program level as well. The Never-Trumpers gave The Department of Energy's Office of Science an additional $42 million. That seems like nothing until you learn that Trump had requested a $900 million reduction. Funding for Community Development Block Grants was kept level despite a $1.5 billion requested reduction. The list goes on. For example, CQ Roll Call reported in early May that: "Trump proposed killing off more than a dozen federal programs in his fiscal 2018 budget outline, but it doesn't appear appropriators are inclined to reduce or eliminate federal funding for any of those line items." Whatever Lola wanted, Lola did not get. Neither did President Trump. Why the President seems happy about this claptrap is the enigma of our times.

Swamp drainers from around the country asked themselves whether the budget results would have been much different if they had voted for Hillary instead of Donald Trump.

The Swamp drainers, for want of a better nickname--Democrat and Republican alike, would cry loud about this face if they believed that anybody would listen. They would scream that the Trumpists need a Party that is there for the regular people in America, not the big shot Trump haters.

Somehow, despite a people's victory in November, it is clear that the Democrats, the Trump-haters in the Republican-majority Congress, the K-Street lobbyists, the donor base, and even the US Chamber of Commerce were able to overpower the administration into accepting not much more than nothing in the 1.1 Trillion Omnibus budget.

The President seems to believe that this group will all be on his side in October and they will pass his 2018 budget or vote to shut down the government. Chances of seeing any Trump programs implemented ever went down by 99% after the Republican cave-in on the Omnibus bill.

The US Chamber of Commerce is not often singled out as being bad guys. Yet, they are scum. Sorry, that is how I see it. Michele Malkin, a noted anti-leftist describes them quite succinctly:

"The U.S. Chamber of Commerce is a politically entrenched synod of special interests. These fat cats do not represent the best interests of American entrepreneurs, American workers, American parents and students, or Americans of any race, class, or age who believe in low taxes and limited government. The chamber's business is the big business of the Beltway, not the business of mainstream America."

I sure wish I had written that. Michele Malkin is one of the good ones.

Can you imagine the fierceness of the snakes in the swamp that are trying to take Donald Trump and the rest of us down with them? Don't ever trust the US Chamber of Commerce. They are anti-American, pro-greed, and as selfish as selfish can be defined.

The type of political party that the anti-leftist swamp-drainers need in order to win back America is definitely not the one controlled today by the weak-kneed, wimpish, elitist establishment Anti-Trump Republicans. They have had the power in the past but have consistently made excuses for not doing what the people voted for.

For years, they deferred to the whims of Barack Obama and his many budgets and his continued excessive spending. This time, they simply took the old Obama budget from 2016, dusted it off, blessed it and said it was good. They snuck this through as if there was not one good and honest Republican left in the Congress, who would stand up and support the needs of the people. Maybe they were right.

Those wanting Trump to stick to his guns would tell any reporter that Republicans have not done it for us. In their first chance to set a budget for the Trump Administration, the supposed Party of Lincoln found our backs and stabbed us again by choice. Lincoln, the first Republican President, and a great one in American History, would have done much better.

This is a betrayal of the people. The values of anti-leftists and like-minded Americans are no longer important to Republicans. Republicans simply cannot be trusted. We know this from history. So, what can we the people do? We can say good-by to the Republican Party. We can end the charade

We cannot afford to trust Republicans ever again. What we need is a solution for regular John Does—those of us out here in Realville, not Plasticville. We need a John Doe solution so that the Republican leadership no longer needs to be important to us, the regular every day citizens of America.

And, so there is a compelling rationale for why the Republican Party must be abandoned in favor of a brand new American Political Party. A great name for this new Party is "The John Doe Party," as we John Does are the people to be represented by this new Party. To repeat, Republicans simply cannot be trusted. In their hearts, Republicans must be wondering why we ever trusted them.

The John Doe Party can be designed to be the party for all the nobodies in America. Gary Cooper and Frank Capra would call these nobodies like you and I, "John Does." That is who we are and the Republicans make sure that we know it every time they have a chance.

The John Doe Party needs to replace the Republican Party as a mainstream political party. Who needs a party that cannot be trusted? Democrats seem happy with the Democratic Party so this essay in this chapter is not directly about them, However, lots of Democrats are John Does like you and I for sure and though they do not trust Republicans, they would more than likely welcome a change to an open and honest group who have their best interests at heart. They are sick of dishonest government just as we anti-leftists.

The irony in losing this budget battle is that in November 2016, anti-communist and anti-leftist Americans believed that we had begun the elimination of the Washington swamp simply by electing Donald Trump. Yet, the elite establishment Republicans did not care to hear and absorb the people's clear message.

Anybody working on a solution regarding the US budget in its Omnibus form, would have brought it in long before May 1, and it would be for the people who won. It would not favor a group that had lost the election.

Slimy RINO Republican leaders unfortunately were way too happy with what the Democrats had done for the past eight years. Their budget showed an affinity for funding Obamacare, funding the baby killing Planned Parenthood, funding Sanctuary Cities, and bringing more "refugees" into America—and of course living without a secure Southern border with an impenetrable and beautiful wall—along with many other dictates from their Trump-hating donors and the special interests on K Street deep in the heart of the swamp.

Of course, the Republican Party for years has turned on its base whenever it was convenient. This is nothing new. Now, while they turn on the people who elected the President, they do so by joining Democrats in demeaning President Trump. They have decided to not permit the President or the people to gain the fruits of their election victory over the Democrats and the swamp establishment.

Too many Republicans in powerful positions hate President Trump more than they hate terrorists and more than they fear that one day they may be thrown out of office. The people therefore must show strength. We must act to shut-down Republican leaders by creating a new Party and then by denying these traitors the right to represent the people ever again.

The John Doe Party is the vehicle to get America right again. Republican leaders abhor the people's trust in Donald Trump, and have served themselves rather than their constituents. They will not be missed, even by the President. And, so the people, the John Does like you and I in the real world must join in to shut the Republican Elite out of any new party that we may form and any new government that we may elect.

Americans do not have to keep taking it on the chin. We have a real choice –**The John Doe Party.**

The immortal Gary Cooper would never let us down. Let's all try to see "Meet John Doe" soon. Viewing this classic movie will assure us that the Washington elites have not served the John Does or Jane Does of America for many, many years. We can change that. We can be the John Doe Club, the John Doe Movement, and the John Doe Party that wins America back for Americans.

When we meet John Doe in the great Capra movie, we will all better understand what being an American is all about! John Doe Democrats and John Doe Republicans, who have seen both political parties abandon the people, will have a choice once again.

It won't be easy but Americans can do anything. It is time to dump the Party of Lincoln. Lincoln would be ashamed of them and demand nothing less to protect his name. Republicans no longer are worthy of our trust, and we, the John Does of America matter.

Let's quickly bring on the John Doe Party

Chapter 4 introduces John Doe, as portrayed by Gary Cooper in the movie. What an inspiring thought! Enjoy as you turn the page.

# Chapter 4  Meet John Doe

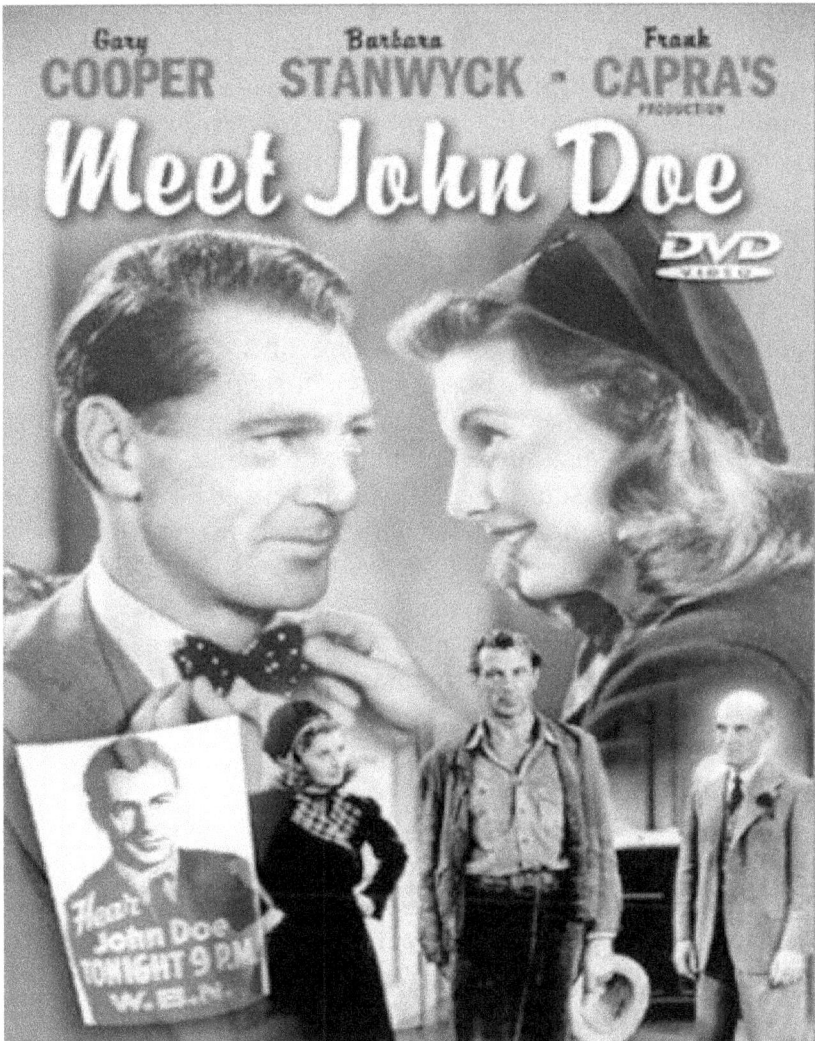

## You'll wish John Doe were your neighbor!

Mostly everybody of today knows what a great actor Jimmy Stewart was as his movies captured the imagination and the hearts of box-office regulars for many years. Then, when his movies such as It's a

Wonderful Life began to be shown regularly around Christmas time, more Jimmy Stewart fans than ever appeared. James Maitland Stewart lived to be 89 years old (May 20, 1908 – July 2, 1997). Many, such as I wish he were still here to help us by his movies, to do the right thing,

Besides being George Bailey in "It's a Wonderful Life," Stewart was also Mr. Smith in "Mr. Smith Goes to Washington." The latter is another great Capra film that gets you right where your heart beats. It is an American political comedy-drama film directed by Frank Capra, starring Jean Arthur and James Stewart (Jimmy Stewart), and featuring movie greats Claude Rains and Edward Arnold.

This particular film is about a newly appointed United States Senator who fights against a corrupt political system, and was written by Sidney Buchman, based on Lewis R. Foster's unpublished story "The Gentleman from Montana". [4] The film was controversial when it was first released, but was also successful at the box office, and made Stewart a major movie star. It is in the same vein as the great movie "Meet John Doe," a bunch of great films in which good triumphs over evil. Wouldn't that be nice in real life?

Most people if given the opportunity to meet John Doe as portrayed by Gary Cooper in the film of the same name would spend little time in saying:

## It would be a pleasure!

One would think there could never be another Jimmy Stewart. But, if there were, his name would be Gary Cooper, another tall, lummox-like simply great guy. Gary Cooper did not live as long as those he portrayed as he made his peace with his maker on May 13, 1961 in Beverly Hills, CA. He could churn a heart just like Jimmy Stewart. They were two of a kind and none have come after them.

The notion of the John Doe Party comes from the John Doe Movement which comes from the movie "Meet John Doe."

One of the most famous quotes of the movie is from a letter sent by Gary Cooper before he actually became John Doe. Like many

Americans today, today, this Mr. Doe had fallen on hard times and hoped his life could have meaning in his planned death. Here it is:

*"Below is a letter which reached my desk this morning. It's a commentary on what we laughingly call a civilized world.*

*"Dear Miss Mitchell: Four years ago, I was fired out of my job. Since then, I haven't been able to get another one. At first, I was sore at the state administration because it's on account of the slimy politics here we have all this unemployment. But in looking around, it seems the whole world is goin' to pot. So in protest, I'm goin' to commit suicide by jumping off the City Hall roof.*

*"Signed, a disgusted American citizen. John Doe.*

## First Old Time Movie Review

What I am about to present here for your reading pleasure is an old-time movie review of what in my opinion and the opinion of millions of movie goers, is one of the finest movies ever produced. Its title is true but to the point: "Meet John Doe." It has great meaning in this book. Thank you for indulging me for a better explanation of the character, John Doe. In the words, of Bosley Crowthe, let's go meet John Doe right now:

Bosley Crowthe, a great writer for the NY Times, back when the Grey Lady was actually reporting news rather than fabricating fake news for a political agenda, felt compelled to do his best to describe political corruption and how goodness has a chance to prevail over badness. I love stories like this. I think you will too.

Where are NYT columnists today with the gumption of Bosley Crowther? Even the NYT back before I was born thought this movie was special. But admittedly, it was not after they had signed-up to be the lead dogs for the party of tyranny, treachery and treason. Yes, I mean the Democrat Party. But, it is still debatable today whether the Times is really the political party and the Democrats are merely playing along to get along. Regardless, here is this great review folks from when the Times was actually the Times:

## 'Meet John Doe,' an Inspiring Lesson in Americanism, Opened at the Rivoli and Hollywood Theatres -- "The Roundup' and 'Mr. Dynamite' Also Here

By BOSLEY CROWTHER

Published: March 13, 1941

**[In 1941, America was the agenda of the patriots]**

"Call him Joe Doakes or George Spelvin or just the great American yap—he is still the backbone of this country and as sturdy a citizen as there is. You've seen him at the ball parks, on buses, at county fairs and political rallies from coast to coast. You've even caught glimpses of him—and seen him squarely, too—in films once and again. But now you will see him about as clearly as Hollywood has ever made him out in Frank Capra's and Robert Riskin's superlative "Meet John Doe," which had its local première last evening at the Rivoli and Hollywood Theatres—you and countless other John Does.

For, in spite of a certain prolixity and an ending which is obviously a sop, this is by far the hardest-hitting and most trenchant picture on the theme of democracy that the Messrs. Capra and Riskin have yet made—and a glowing tribute to the anonymous citizen, too.

Actually, this is not our first introduction to John Doe. Mr. Capra has already presented him under the names of Longfellow Deeds and Jefferson Smith, the fellows, you remember, who went to town and to Washington, respectively. He is the honest and forthright fellow—confused, inconsistent but always sincere—who believes in the basic goodness of people and has the courage to fight hard for principles. When he went to town, he was fighting for a vague but comprehensible social ideal; in Washington, his adversaries were those who would use the United States Senate for corrupt and venal purposes.

But now, under the pseudonym of John Doe—John Willoughby is his real name—he finds himself confronted with a much more sinister and pertinent foe: the man—or, rather, the class—that would obtain dictatorial control by preying upon the democratic impulses and good-will of the people of the land. In substance, the Messrs. Capra and Riskin are hinting broadly at the way this country might conceivably fall into the hands of a ruthless tyrant. It could happen here, they say—if it were not for the American John Doe.

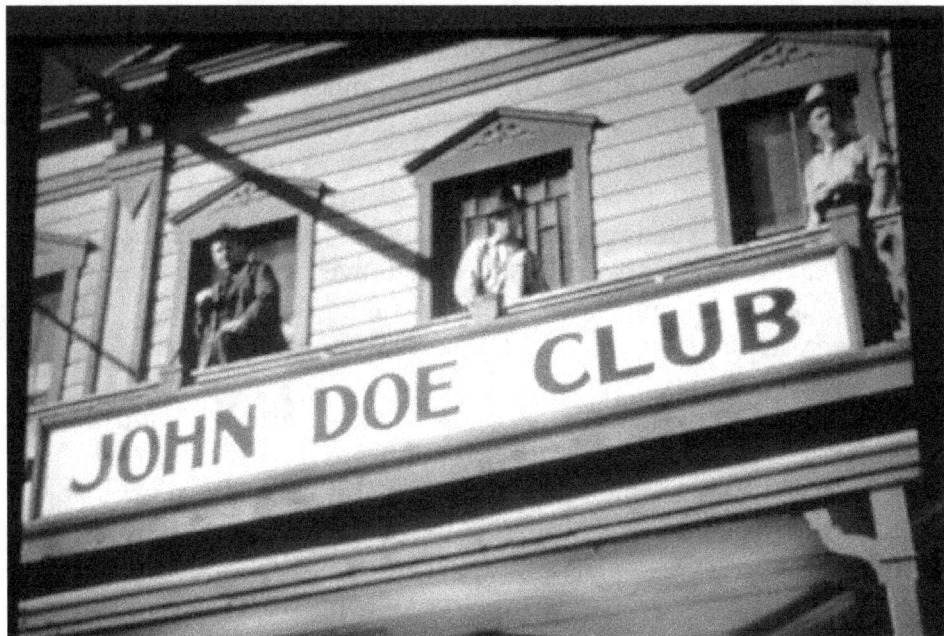

For their story is that of a young fellow, a genial and aimless tramp, who is hoaxed into playing the role of a cynical social firebrand for the sake of a newspaper stunt. At first, he lolls in luxury while articles ag'in this and that are ghost-written for him and printed in the aggressive, unscrupulous sheet. Then, under the pleasantly romantic influence of his beautiful "ghost," he goes on the radio with a stirring and encouraging appeal to the "little man" for brotherly love and democratic good-will.

Immediately, and by virtue of his simple, sincere address, he becomes a national hero, the messiah for little people all around. John Doe Clubs are formed, a spontaneous "movement" gets under way. But then the guiding hand behind the whole set-up appears: the owner of the paper, a Napoleonic industrialist, indicates his intention of using the voting strength of the clubs to bludgeon his way into power. And, at this point, John Doe takes the bit in his teeth and gives courageous battle. The outcome is not resolved; in the end, John Doe is almost licked. But so, too, is his opponent, and an ideal has been preserved.

With an excellent script by Mr. Riskin—overwritten in many spots, it is true—Mr. Capra has produced a film, which is eloquent with affection for gentle people, for the plain, unimpressive little people who want reassurance and faith. Many of his camera devices are magnificent in the scope of their suggestion, and always he tells his story well, with his customary expert spacing of comedy and serious drama. Only space prevents us from enthusing loudly about individual "touches."

And his cast is uniformly excellent. Gary Cooper, of course, is "John Doe" to the life and in the whole—shy, bewildered, non-aggressive, but a veritable tiger when aroused. Barbara Stanwyick plays the "ghost" and, incidentally, the dea ex machina with a proper brittleness, and Edward Arnold is, as usual, the diabolically disarming tycoon.

In supporting roles James Gleason makes a forbiddingly hard-boiled managing editor whose finer instincts are revealed in a superb drunk scene; and Walter Brennan, Harry Holman and Regis Toomey are distinguished among a host of character bits.
John Doe may not be the most profound or incisive fellow in this cross-purposed world of ours today. But he has an inspiring message for all good Americans. And he is charming company. We most heartily suggest you make his acquaintance at once.

**MEET JOHN DOE,** screen play by Robert Riskin; from an original story by Richard Connell and Robert Presnell; produced and directed by Frank Capra and released through Warner Brothers. At the Rivoli and Hollywood Theaters.

"John Doe" . . . . . Gary Cooper
Ann Mitchell . . . . . Barbara Stanwyck
Colonel . . . . . Walter Brennan
D. B. Norton . . . . . Edward Arnold
Connell . . . . . James Gleason
Mayor Lovett . . . . . Gene Lockhart
Beany . . . . . Irving Bacon
Tim Sheldon . . . . . Rod LaRocque
Mrs. Mitchell . . . . . Spring Byington
Weston . . . . . Pierre Watkin
Barrington . . . . . Russell Simpson
Bennett . . . . . Stanley Andrews
Spencer . . . . . Andrew Toombes
Mike . . . . . Pat Flaherty

Mug . . . . . Gene Morgan
Mrs. Webster . . . . . Mrs. Gardner Crane
Bert . . . . . Regis Toomey
Mayor Hawkins . . . . . Harry Holman
Bert's Wife . . . . . Ann Doran
Mayor's Wife . . . . . Sara Edwards
Pop Dwyer . . . . . Aldrich Bowker
Political Manager . . . . . Ed Stanley
Red . . . . . Bennie Bartlett
Mattie . . . . . Bess Flowers
Sourpuss . . . . . J. Farrell McDonald
Dan . . . . . Sterling Holloway
Radio Announcer . . . . . Knox Manning
Signpainter . . . . . Gary Owen

Get your own copy of the DVD from the company that prints and promotes my books—amazon.com. https://www.amazon.com/Meet-John-Doe-Gary-Cooper/dp/B00005RERN

If you'd like to find more of my books, it too is easy, **amazon.com/author/brianwkelly**

Enjoy!

I love the notion of John Doe. I am not kidding about the thought for good Americans to again put forth the notion of a political party for John Doe's, which of course can save us from the dishonesty of the Republican Party. What a great idea! I am glad I thought of it but without you and a few people who have a lot in their pockets, we will be forced to beg Republicans for alms all of our lives.

That's why I love the notion of The John Doe Party!

If Gary Cooper were alive today and he really were the John Doe from the movie, he would help us get through this dark period of history just as John Does did back in the movie. To help you get inspired to create the John Doe Party and John Doe Clubs and other John Doe affiliates, here is the national radio address delivered by John Doe during the movie. Notice like today's Town Hall Meetings, those with corruption on their mind had no problem heckling Mr. Doe. Here it is

John Doe Delivers National Radio Address

http://www.americanrhetoric.com/MovieSpeeches/moviespeechmeetj
ohndoe.html

John Doe:

Ladies and Gentlemen, I am the man you all know as John Doe. I took
that name because it seems to describe -- because it seems to describe the
average man, and that's me -- and that's me.

Well, it was me -- before I said I was gonna jump off the City Hall roof
at midnight on Christmas Eve. Now, I guess I'm not average any more.
Now, I'm getting all sorts of attention, from big shots, too -- the mayor
and governor, for instance. They don't like those articles I've been
writing.

**D.B. Norton:** You're an impostor, young fella. That's a pack of lies you're telling. Who wrote that speech for you?

**Announcer:** Ladies and Gentlemen, the disturbance you just heard was caused by someone in the audience who tried to heckle Mr. Doe. The speech will continue.

**John Doe:** Well, people like the Governor -- people like the Governor -- and that fella there can -- can stop worrying. I'm not gonna talk about them. I'm gonna talk about us, the average guys, the John Does.

If anybody should ask you what the average John Doe is like, you couldn't tell him because he's a million and one things. He's Mr. Big and Mr. Small. He's simple and he's wise. He's inherently honest, but he's got a streak of larceny in his heart. He seldom walks up to a public telephone without shoving his finger into the slot to see if somebody left a nickel there.

He's the man the ads are written for. He's the fella everybody sells things to. He's Joe Doakes, the world's greatest stooge and the world's greatest strength.

Yes, sir -- Yes, sir, we're a great family, the John Does. We are the meek who are -- who are supposed to inherit the earth. You'll find us everywhere. We raise the crops; we dig the mines, work the factories, keep the books, fly the planes and drive the busses. And when a cop yells: "Stand back there, you!" He means us, the John Does!

We have existed since time began. We built the pyramids. We saw Christ crucified, pulled the oars for Roman emperors, sailed the boats for Columbus, retreated from Moscow with Napoleon and froze with Washington at Valley Forge.

Yes, sir. We've been in there dodging left hooks since before history began to walk. In our struggle for freedom we've hit the canvas many a time, but we always bounced back! Because we're the people -- and we're tough.

They've started a lot of talk about free people going soft -- that we can't take it. That's a lot of hooey! A free people can beat the world at anything, from war to tiddle-de-winks, if we all pull in the same direction.

I know a lot of you are saying "What can I do? I'm just a little punk. I don't count." Well, you're dead wrong! The little punks have always counted because in the long run the character of a country is the sum total of the character of its little punks.

But, we've all got to get in there and pitch. We can't win the old ballgame unless we have teamwork. And that's where every John Doe comes in. It's up to him to get together with his teammates. And your teammate, my friend, is the guy next door to you. Your neighbor -- he's a terribly important guy that guy next door. You're gonna need him and he's gonna need you, so look him up. If he's sick, call on him. If he's hungry, feed him. If he's out of a job, find him one.

To most of you, your neighbor is a stranger, a guy with a barkin' dog and high fence around him. Now, you can't be a stranger to any guy that's on your own team. So, tear down the fence that separates you. Tear down the fence and you'll tear down a lot of hates and prejudices. Tear down all the fences in the country and you'll really have teamwork.

I know a lot of you are saying to yourselves, "He's askin' for a miracle to happen. He's expectin' people to change all of a sudden. Well, you're wrong. It's no miracle. It's no miracle because I see it happen once every year. And so do you -- at Christmas time. There's somethin' swell about the spirit of Christmas, to see what it does to people, all kinds of people.

Now, why can't that spirit, that same, warm Christmas spirit last the whole year around? Gosh, if it ever did, if each and every John Doe would make that spirit last 365 days out of the year, we'd develop such strength, we'd create such a tidal wave of good will that no human force could stand against it. Yes sir, my friends, the meek can only inherit the earth when the John Doe's start lovin' their neighbors.

You better start right now. Don't wait till the game is called on account of darkness. Wake up, John Doe. You're the hope of the world. --- End of John Doe's National Radio Address

## Here is another wonderful review of the movie:

http://www.midnightpalace.com/film-reviews/film-review-meet-john-doe-1941-2

**MEET JOHN DOE (1941)**
**Film Title: Meet John Doe**         **Year: 1941**
**Studio: Warner Brothers**          **Silent or Talkie: Talkie**
**Genre: Drama**                     **Starring:**
**Gary Cooper**                      **Barbara Stanwyck**
**Edward Arnold**                    **Walter Brennan**

## Second Review

Frank Capra readily admitted that he thought Barbara Stanwyck wasn't good enough to be an actress when he first met her as a young girl. During their first meeting, she lashed out at him verbally. Having been kicked around Hollywood for months, Stanwyck was fed up with all the mind games and empty promises. Her tirade was the culmination of many frustrating meetings with directors, producers and advisors. Stanwyck accused Capra of wasting her time. She felt that he wasn't really interested in her abilities and only took the meeting out of professional courtesy.

Her behavior only solidified Capra's opinion of her as a "loose cannon". It wasn't until Stanwyck's husband (at the time) Frank Fay called Capra and demanded that he see test footage of her before making any snap decisions that he changed his mind. Capra was sold on her and cast her in his 1930 film Ladies of Leisure. He would direct her in a total of five films, the last being 1941's Meet John Doe opposite Gary Cooper, who accepted the role without reading the script because he wanted to work with Stanwyck.

Stanwyck is Ann Mitchell, a writer for The Bulletin newspaper. When publisher D.B. Norton (Edward Arnold) takes over, he changes the name to The New Bulletin and demands a new format. This prompts the managing editor, Henry Connell (James Gleason) to fire Ann. The new paper needs stories that light a fire under people and Connell finds Ann's writing to be anything but exciting. Though she begs and pleads to keep her job, Connell insists that she finish her last column, collect her final paycheck and leave. Never one to back down easily, Ann has a brainstorm. She writes a column that includes a letter supposedly sent in by a man named "John Doe."

In the letter, Doe rants about the state of the world and the lack of goodwill in modern-day society. He ends his rant by vowing to commit suicide from the City Hall on Christmas Eve as a show of principle for his beliefs. In reality, there is no John Doe and Ann never received any such letter. She cooked up the scenario to give Connell the fireworks he wanted. Initially skeptical, Connell wants no parts of the publicity stunt until scores of people respond dramatically to the printed letter. It's then that he realizes the gold mine in front of him. Ann, as the author of the new recipe for success, demands her job back and $1,000 bonus.

Connell complies and the paper immerses itself in the John Doe phenomenon. Now there's only one small detail to satisfy. Since there is no physical John Doe, they must figure out a way to find someone willing to pose as the mystery man. A crowd of men show up at the newspaper office, all claiming to be John Doe. Ann and Connell bring them in one by one to scrutinize. The majority are vagrants looking for a quick buck or an easy meal.

FRANK CAPRA'S PRODUCTION · GARY COOPER ... BARBARA STANWYCK .. "MEET JOHN DOE" Produced at Warner Brothers Studio

After hours of sifting through weathered faces, a man named John Willoughby (Gary Cooper) presents himself. Ann immediately perks up at the sight of the interesting prospect. Willoughby has not come to "audition" for the role of Doe, but rather in search of a job for himself and his friend "The Colonel" (Walter Brennan). The two are drifters.

Willoughby is a former pitcher who lost his career to an arm injury and The Colonel is more concerned with jumping freight trains from state to state. When Ann asks Willoughby about his willingness to assume the identity of John Doe, his reluctance is fueled by The Colonel's insistence that financial gain will only ruin him and attract the attention of "heelots" (The Colonel's term for bill collectors and salesman who prey on people with money).

After some reassuring words, Willoughby relents and agrees to take on the new persona. The paper continues to churn out letters supposedly written by Doe, in which he confronts every issue plaguing the common man. The ideal begins to catch on around the country and "John Doe" becomes a folk hero of sorts.

Bulletin publisher Norton soon devises a plan to use this to his political advantage. He instructs Ann to work directly with him and commissions her to pen a radio speech for Doe. The speech, Norton believes, will put their "discovery" over the top and grab the attention of every Tom, Dick and Harry (also known as the real voters). Ann has difficulty writing the speech. She toils for hours at home, throwing away drafts and losing her confidence in the process. Her mother (played by Spring Byington) suggests that she draw inspiration from her late father's diary. This proves to be the winning ingredient.

As Doe is preparing to make his radio debut, a columnist from competing publication The Chronicle tries to pay him in exchange for reading a different letter over the air. The Chronicle letter has Doe exposing the Bulletin's hoax. Though he agrees to do it (knowing that the payoff money will allow him to have his arm fixed), he bails on the deal at the last minute and reads Ann's original script instead. Doe is secretly in love with Ann and he knows that betraying her trust would shatter any chance he may have.

He begins to deliver in a shaky voice, nervously gripping the microphone stand and stumbling over ordinary words. However, by mid-speech he seems to boast a newfound confidence. Meanwhile, The Colonel keeps motioning towards an open door as a means of escape. Doe ignores his friend's suggestions and continues speaking until every last word has been proclaimed. The emotion overwhelms him and he bolts through the side door to run away as soon as he finishes.

Now resuming life as John Willoughby, he and The Colonel stop off for donuts in another town. Willoughby notices a truck driving by with a sign that reads "The John Doe Club". Ann and Norton catch up to Willoughby and try to persuade him to continue his artificial crusade.

He claims to want no part of the ruse or Ann's proposal of a national speaking tour. Suddenly, members of a local John Doe Club ask to speak with Willoughby (who they think is John Doe). He listens apprehensively to their stories of goodwill and newly formed friendships, all based around the ideals of his simple message of faith.

When Willoughby realizes the impact he's made, he resumes life as John Doe of his own free will. They embark on the speaking tour.

Doe is now completely in love with Ann and approaches her mother for advice on how to tell her. Meanwhile, Ann has gone to Norton's home for a meeting with various political figures who are trying to organize a John Doe convention. The convention will pack the numerous John Doe clubs from around the country into one venue for a speech to end all speeches.

Norton's plan is to pull the strings from behind the scenes by way of a strategically written script in which Doe announces his own political party. He will naturally name Norton as his candidate of choice for the President of the United States. Ann is turned off by the idea of cheapening the movement but seems to have little say in the matter. Connell also disapproves of the tactic. He gets drunk and spills the beans to Doe, who storms off to Norton's house for a confrontation.

Once there, he notices Ann among the planning committee and promises to uphold the original message of hope despite Norton's attempt to capitalize on it. Ann runs after Doe and tries to go with him, but he ignores her and goes to the convention alone. As he begins to make his speech, Norton shows up with his committee and exposes Doe as a fraud.

The crowd of supporters becomes a crowd of disillusioned people who turn hostile. Having no opportunity to tell his side of the story, Doe is chastised and takes to the streets as a loner. Ann is guilt-ridden and worried about Doe's safety. She has fallen in love with him and feels remorse for starting the charade. In a moment of panic, it becomes evident to all that Doe may prove his sincerity by acting out the intentions of his first letter.

Gary Cooper and Barbara Stanwyck would make one more film together in 1941, Ball of Fire. Cooper already had a good amount of film work under his belt. His career began in the 1920s, playing bit parts and doing extra work, though he went uncredited for his first 12 roles. His first credited role was in 1926's Lightnin' Wins, where he received third billing.

He would go uncredited for a few more roles in the latter half of the 20s, but by the end of decade, he was making films every year and would continue to make films every year (with the exception of 1960) up until his death in 1961. He is often associated with western plots and cowboys, but also remembered as Lou Gehrig in The Pride of the Yankees.

In this film, Cooper worked very well as the bumpkin-turned-activist. He perfected a technique of keeping his eyes low and glancing around quickly, as if confused out of innocence. The simplistic nature of his character made for a high level of believability. Cooper became John Doe. He was the embodiment of the ordinary man struggling to make it in a world dominated by big business.

Director Frank Capra must have noticed those qualities in Cooper from the beginning. He'd worked with Cooper once before in 1936's Mr. Deeds Goes to Town and wanted no one else for the role of Doe. Stanwyck was her usual unforgettable self. She often echoed her personal life through the characters she portrayed and Ann Mitchell was no exception. Her first show of ambition came through immediately, refusing to accept the loss of her job. With quick thinking, she orchestrated a way to be needed. Stanwyck always had the ability to command respect and make the viewer cry in the same sequence. It's a rare quality that few have mastered over the course of film history.

She was as tough as she was fragile, though when her glass jaw started to show, she guarded it with the fists of a champion. Like many classic films, the supporting cast of Meet John Doe was of particular importance. Walter Brennan as The Colonel was annoying, but in a good way. The Colonel was supposed to be annoying. He was paranoid, overly protective and a bit egotistical.

So, in that respect, Brennan played him in the best possible way. The viewer wants the John Doe movement to prosper and The Colonel's condescending attitude is anything but welcome. All in all, Meet John Doe is a great yarn about the foundation of humanity and how collectively, we can make the world a better place.

# On Video

Meet John Doe is currently in the public domain. Having said that, there is no one superior DVD release. Like many films without a copyright, it has been released by various companies, mostly without any restoration or extras. For that reason alone, one release cannot be recommended over another. However, you will still find a link at the bottom of this review to purchase a copy.

As a side note, it should be mentioned that Meet John Doe is a film with a powerful message and deserves to be picked up by a studio for that reason, if not for its entertainment value alone. This film should be preserved for many future generations.

# Conclusion

What hasn't already been said? Gary Cooper, Barbara Stanwyck and a story about society at its most basic level – it could only be memorable. The public has seen horror and tolerated violence.

At the very least, we can spend a little over two hours remembering what it means to be civil. Everyone knows a "John Doe" and some of us are "John Doe". There are bits of comedy mixed in to soften the harsh blow of reality, but in reality, the message comes through loud and clear courtesy of Hollywood's elite.

https://www.amazon.com/Meet-John-Doe-Gary-Cooper/dp/B00005RERN

Now that we know we are the John Does in America, we need to realize that when we organize, just like the John Doe in Meet John Doe, we can move mountains.

"If it is worth dying for then it is worth living for"

In the next chapter, we again examine the Republican party and its new propensity to lie rather than represent the American people. We the John Does of America must understand that the Republicans are way off the mark today and rather than join them, we must join together to replace them as the respectable political party in America.

# Chapter 5 Why Lie?

## Republicans may be infrequent liars but liars nonetheless

I hope you enjoy this off-center introduction to the chapter that offers some rationale about why the Republicans choose to lie way too often to the American people. Democrats have been and continue to be incessant liars and I cannot recall a lie that they may have ever told for a good purpose.

"If you tell a lie big enough and keep repeating it, people will eventually come to believe it."

-- Dr . Joseph Goebbels

Anti-leftists such as I, even if we are Democrats by registration, long ago hitched our wagons to the Republican Party because Republicans at least talked about the great values of America and Americans, whereas the Democrat message was always spent in hope of duping regular citizens. Republicans once talked the talk and walked the walk. That was until recent years when they began to play footsie with Barack Obama on budget matters and now with Trump, their little feet are still moving towards Obama's feet but that is completely unacceptable to America and Americans.

Then one day, the Republicans decided it was OK to lie.

## Can it be for beer?

My brother Joe Kelly, who once was the best Food Service Supervisor that the VA Hospital in Wilkes-Barre, PA ever had in their employ, scheduled his life well enough that he actually could take real vacations. On a particular vacation with me, his beautiful wife Diane could not accompany him because of a work conflict (She is a nurse). Joe asked a friend Bill Kepics, a progressive liberal but a nice guy, nonetheless, to accompany us a conference that I had to attend for business in San Francisco.

A great friend of mine, Gerry Rodski had offered to share a room so that the four of us could make the trek while just two of us would be attending the tech sessions at the conference. The plan was to meet for Happy Hour each night of the San Francisco experience. It was great. It was like a fishing trip for four without having to go fishing.

My brother sat in on one tech session that I conducted at the conference. He is four years younger than I and he is a handsome man for sure. I had written a book called AS/400 Data Warehousing (DW) and the session was intended to describe the rudiments of the AS/400 computer solution for DW. It was well received.

We had a few minutes after the event and I offered to sign any books that those in the audience brought forward. As that process began, an attractive young lady called out that she would like her book signed by Joseph Kelly, my brother.

Other young tech ladies did the same. Joe kindly signed the books but resisted the under current as he was a happily married man. Mr. Rodski was in the room as the DW topic was new to him but Mr. Kepics was not present. Kepics would have enjoyed the female entreaties if they were towards him as he remains single but still finds the opposite sex very attractive as they do him.

That is just the exciting warm-up to the real Why Lie story.

On the second or third day of the conference, my brother Joe was no longer coming to sessions. He was out and about enjoying the lively streets of San Francisco with his best friend in life, Bill Kepics. Joe and the Kepster (Bill Kepics' nickname) took the cable car to Fisherman's Wharf and had a ball.

Gerry Rodski and I were slugging it out with the tech presenters at the conference trying to get as much knowledge as we could on the new elements of the system so we would be more effective when we returned from the conference. My brother and the Kepster came back after a day of fun with a picture to commemorate their day at the Wharf. The pic is shown below"

As you can see, the picture is of a reasonably-dressed pan-handler with a different sort of message. It was so obvious and so unusual that my brother asked his buddy to snap this picture and he told me that he generously donated and conversed with the honest funds-seeking broker. That's Joe in the background with the yellow package and his head cropped. For those viewing in b/w, Joe lines up perfectly with the Why Lie sign.

The pose may have cost a bit more but, nonetheless, we were all intrigued. The next day after early conference sessions, we all went to experience the man with the sign.

There he was unabashed in his iniquity and apparently ready to face as many days as he could to gain recompense and eventually some good beer for his absolute honesty. The passers-by were all intrigued. He was asking for money like all pan-handlers do. He was sitting back on a small bridge against the rail with a pan that looked like a tambourine and a sign created by a magic marker that read: "Why lie? It's for beer!"

Though his mission was not necessarily noble, he was a lot more truthful than the Republican leadership of today who lie through their teeth to the people that the people's agenda is their agenda. Nothing can be further from the truth. Their agenda is to please their big rich donors and lobbyists and the people are not even on their radar. They could use a little honesty such as "Why Lie? It's for beer?" But, they don't ever fess up. They just do the bidding of those to whom they are beholden and it is not the people.

By the way, before I continue about the lying Republicans, I have since found a number of other pictures of people who use Why Lie as their honesty catch phrase. Would it not be nice if Republicans said Why Lie? I am now an honest representative! See an honest Republican Representative on the next page. He is definitely the honorable so and so from such and such. I

I could not resist showing this potentially honest bloke in the spirit of the original San Francisco Why Lie!

Which district of your state does this fella represent?

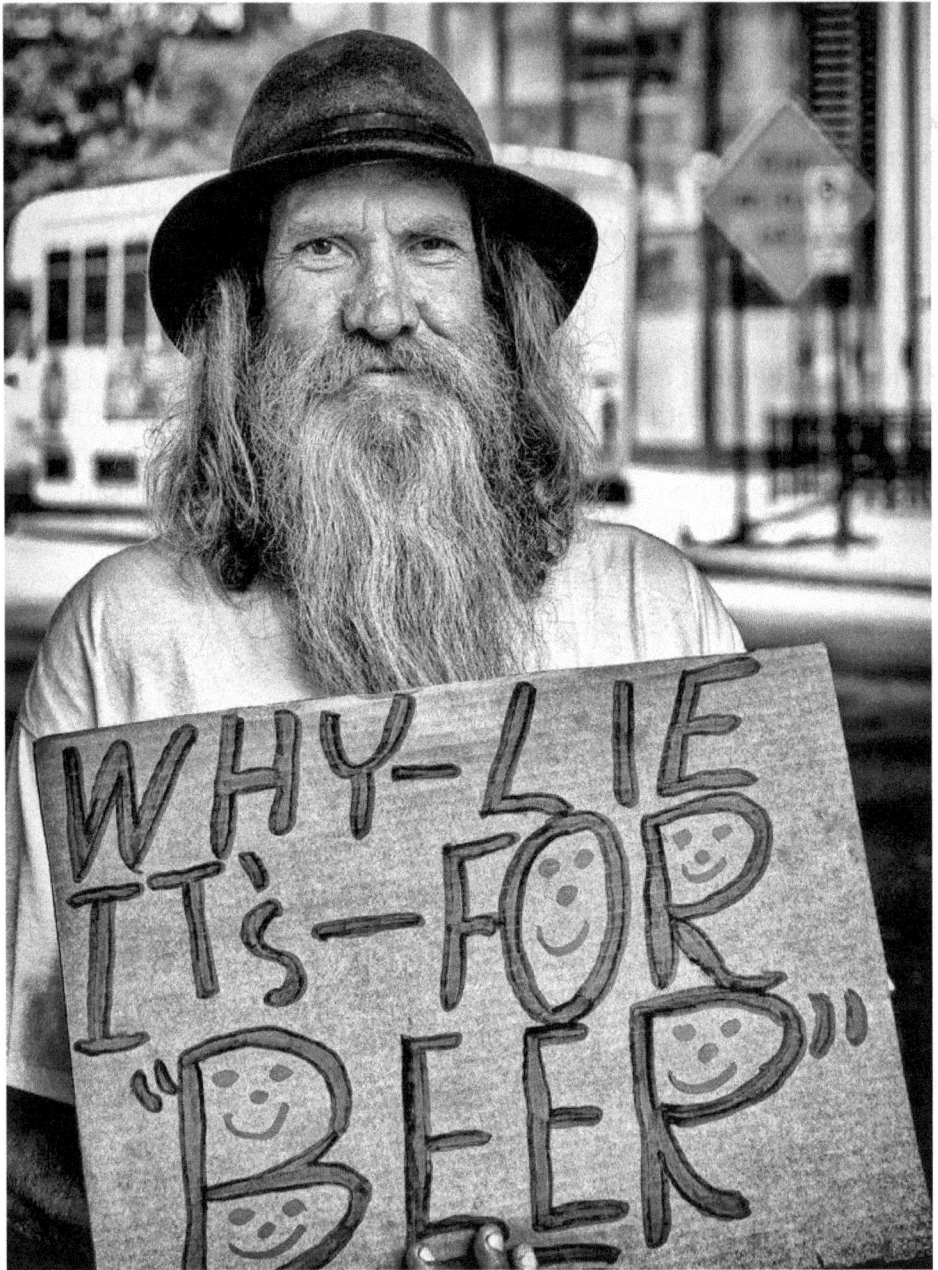

The honorable so and so from such and such! The true look of an American politician

Every now and then a good Republican shows up and takes on the lying leadership of the party. For example, in March 2017, Louis Gohmert had had enough of the lies regarding the repeal of Obamacare.

He was on Fox and Friends and he was very open while detailing how Obamacare had hurt the majority of Americans, especially the elderly. He said that it appears the GOP leadership's current strategy is "we're gonna hurt our elderly folks a little more, but don't worry."

Gohmert is one of my favorites. He is a proud member of the House Freedom Caucus, and he is interested in a real repeal and replacement not a package of lies representing a watered-down version of Obamacare.

According to Gohmert, this was the lie: "We can't do what you guys want to do because the parliamentarian won't allow us to do it. Now, we can't check with the parliamentarian until we pass the bill in the House, send it to the Senate, and then the parliamentarian can rule." Gohmert says these are all lies. Why lie?

A Great Congress Person Louis Gohmert

If this chapter introduction were written by a Trump-hating promulgator of fake news, you can bet that they would ignore the facts and affix the dates of the encounter so as to depict that my brother's discovery, "Why

Lie," from Fisherman's Wharf was really a young Donald Trump in the
months before he got his family grub stake leading to his fortune. Once
upon a time, it was just Democrats who lied. Now, Republicans get
enough lies told just fast enough to push their donor agenda.

## Why Lie? The people would not reelect me!

When a drunken pan handler on the streets of San Francisco has more
class than sitting Republican members of the House of Representatives
and the US Senate, we have come a long way from the patriot days
when honest men spoke with honest men in the legislature and then
later discussed matters in the town tavern. The quaff added to the

honesty for sure. The City Tavern in Philadelphia in the days of Ben Franklin (on prior page) often filled the bill for the early Patriots:

When Donald Trump ran for office he spoke the truth in all ways, even about things, which in the future he might not have control. But, why would he ever think that the Republicans in the House and the Senate, if they were honest representatives of the people, would consider lining up with the Democrats against America to smear and besmirch its President. Yet, that is what this President has experienced. How well would you stand up in such an environment where your enemies remained your enemies and your supposed friends were more treacherous than your known enemies. I admire Donald Trump for his tenacity but I want to see no chumminess with the swamp.

Welcome to the one-time world when we could trust Republicans to do the right thing. It ain't going to happen again because this dishonest opportunistic Congress thinks it does not make enough money per year to avoid falling into hell by acquiescing to the temptation of the bribes of the donors and the promises from lobbyist operatives for an after-Congress life with a huge salary.

It is a tough life for our President whose mission is to drain the swamp of such representatives and who finds the Republican-led Congress operating against him from their HQ in the swamp on K street and elsewhere. The people must save the President from the swamp. But, the President must also resist the temptation of the swamp.

Picture yourself as Donald Trump, who comes in with a team of swamp suckers and the equipment needed for a big-time wholesome drain job. We see already in just a few months that those depending on the swamp for their excesses in life do not like it one bit at all. They have lined up against Trump's legislation and executive orders and appear to be against Trump being able to do anything—including breathing.

An unacceptable solution for dishonesty in government may be to pay members of Congress about $10 million per year instead of $170,000. Even this probably would not be enough. The $200,000 per year with expenses that they currently pocket ought to be enough or they should get another job.

The honorable so and so from such and such has a lot of reason to lie. One way of assuring purity of heart is with a lie detector test. If before taking the oath, they can't pass then they should immediately be expunged from office and that seat stays vacant until the next normal election. In fact, they should be put in jail just for thinking about becoming dishonest.

Sometimes as I watch the inconsistent behavior of the president such as on the Omnibus bill and the "Repeal" and Replace that perhaps the big donors or the K-street mafia from the swamp have been able to threaten him or threaten his family in ways that we see only in some of the network TV shows such as Scandal.

My personal fear is that somebody has threatened the President to accept the claptrap he is being fed… or else. And perhaps he is in peril. I hope it is not so but I have an active mind. I would not put it past desperate people whose beloved swamp is being drained to attack our President and threaten his family.

## Why Lie? You know why?

You see the analogy I am sure between the drunken panhandler who won't lie on Fisherman's wharf and those drunk with power in Washington. Legislators excuse themselves for their lies. Their honesty is a ruse. The guys we elect, lie regularly to protect their next opportunity to be reelected regardless of its impact on the country. What if they told the truth? What would it sound like? Nobody would expect any corrupt legislator to actually come out and say something like this but it would sure be refreshing:

"You know I am lying. I know I am lying. Why Lie? It's all I know. I will lie to get my way and I really do not care why you elected me as you will elect me again because I will lie and convince you to elect me. I will be back in office and you can't stop me." I think when hit between the eyes like that we would send such a bum home for good.

Though I see some things I do not like and things happen differently than I would like, I am still on the Trump team. I am confident that President Trump must begin to keep the promises that he made such as:

"We're going to have insurance for everybody," Trump told the Washington Post after the election. Under Trumpcare, according to Trump, people "can expect to have great health care. It will be in much simplified form. Much less expensive and much better."

The new bill passed by the House does not yet come close to the full essence of the Trump promise, but then again, the Republicans in the swamp have told the President that there are two more phases to come. We'll see.

Do you trust Republicans? I think too many of them want to destroy Trump's presidency and in so doing the people's dreams. That's why the John Doe Party is so appealing and so appropriate.

I am not a fan at all of Paul Ryan. He is of the swamp and for the swamp as I see it. The lying he used to preserve Obamacare while calling it a *repeal* makes no sense but the fervor of the lying is remarkable. I would go so far as to say that it has likely surpassed the degree of intensity of the corrupt Gang of Eight immigration bill when Republicans were trying to convince anti-leftists that the bill was the opposite of what it actually was.

Yes, members of the Republican elite swamp government lie right to the people. They think they are smarter than us. We must stop believing them and begin our new party – the John Doe Party.

Would you trust either of these guys?

This picture was taken shortly after Ryan became the Speaker of the House and began to call the shots on the Republican elite agenda. They look too cozy, don't they? Which one do you trust the most / least?

Conservatives and anti-leftists were enraged at Paul Ryan's actions after such a short time holding the power of the purse. He may as well have been Barack H. Obama because he gave the former President even more than Obama expected in a budget funding debacle that lasted far too long and again this year has been extended.  Ironically, both funding bills are for $1.1 Trillion.

## Examples of some really big lies

There were lots of headlines in 2015 decrying this new chumminess between the Speaker and the President. One major headline from Breitbart, describing what the regular Joes on the street thought about the prior Ryan budget resolution before the big Ryan Omnibus debacle of Mayday 2017 goes like this:

## Paul Ryan Betrays America: $1.1 Trillion, 2,000-Plus Page Omnibus Bill Funds 'Fundamental Transformation of America'

Doesn't this sound a lot like Mayday, 2017. Yet, this headline is from December 16, 2015. That is why anti-leftists and the pro Trump crowd are enraged that the Republicans did it again with their Omnibus 2.0 in May 2017. How many times must we get burned by Republicans leaders before we actually fire them and start over. The John Doe Party is a great way to eliminate Republican establishment rule and pull the plug on the Republican side of the swamp.

Steve Bannon, a name we all recognize & Julia Hannon wrote the following lead to their article in December 2016. They needed to express their outrage and the outrage of all the little guys out there who were hoping Ryan would be a much better conservative leader than Boehner. Ryan needs to be fired. Here is what they wrote.:

*Paul Ryan's first major legislative achievement is a total and complete sell-out of the American people masquerading as an appropriations bill.*

*Too harsh, you say? Let the programs, the spending, and the implications speak for themselves.*

This is all old news but it was replayed in front of us again by the Same Paul Ryan on Mayday 2017. Say it ain't so Joe, but it is! You will know them by the scent of the swamp in the air as they go about their business.

There was little talk about a wall in 2014 and 2015, but there was a lot of outrage on President Obama's end run on the Constitution to fund all sorts of illegals and emigres that Trump would eventually promise to shut down. And, for that we all elected him.

You may recall the outrage and the major public attention surrounded Obama's 2014 executive amnesty. While Americans were out of work, the former President's 2012 amnesty quietly continued to churn out work permits and federal benefits for hundreds of thousands of illegal aliens. It is still going on. The Obama Ryan team funded the 2012 amnesty in its entirety without asking for anything from the Democrats. It also funded the euphemistic "Dreamers"—aka, those illegal immigrants who came to the country as minors.

There was not even an attempt by Ryan to minimize the impact of the Obama unconstitutional activities. There was no language for example, to limit the use of funds and prohibit them from being used for DACA, Deferred Action for Childhood Arrivals, which as we know is a source for many of the gang members now in the country. Ryan funded the 700,000 illegal aliens with work permits, as well as the ability to receive tax credits and federal entitlement programs.

Should we trust a speaker of the house who in 2013 said that he believes "that it is his job as a U.S. lawmaker to put himself in the shoes of "the Dreamer who is waiting" and work to find legislative solutions to his or her problems." Paul Ryan at the same time said nothing about Americans out of work because of illegal immigration.

The Mayday 2017 Omnibus bill funds these same programs and does not offer a dime for the Trump Wall. Speculation is that the staffers of donors and K-Street lobbyists wrote the 2017 Mayday Omnibus, which continues to fund Barack Obama's dream world. Yet, anti-leftists who voted for Trump believed that Republicans were representing us.

Here are the other elements in bullet form as written by Steve Bannon and Julia Hannon. Closer than Chris Christie and Obama hugging on the beach during the aftermath of Hurricane2 Sandy, the new buddy team of Obama and Ryan funded all things Obama at the end of 2015. They continue still:

- **Ryan's Omnibus Fully Funds DACA**
- **Ryan's Omnibus Funds Sanctuary Cities**
- **Ryan's Omnibus Funds All Refugee Programs**

- **Ryan's Omnibus Funds All of the Mideast Immigration Programs That Have Been Exploited by Terrorists in Recent Years**
- **Ryan's Omnibus Funds Illegal Alien Resettlement**
- **Ryan's Omnibus Funds the Release of Criminal Aliens**
- **Ryan's Omnibus Quadruples H-2B Foreign Worker Visas**
- **Ryan's Omnibus Funds Tax Credits for Illegal Aliens**
- **Ryan's Omnibus Locks-In Huge Spending Increases**
- **Ryan's Omnibus Fails to Allocate Funds to Complete the 700-Mile Double-Layer Border Fence That Congress Promised the American People.**

You may recall about ten years ago when Congress lied to the American people and took credit for building a border fence and then never budgeted the funds. This was the 2006 Secure Fence Act. The American people were promised a 700-mile double-layer border fence. It was before Donald Trump began to refer to the beautiful wall. This was just a fence, but a huge fence. People demanded it but we forgot and Congress remembered to forget. OK, they simply lied. Well, Ryan's Omnibus does not even require that funds be allocated to finish the construction of the 700-mile double-layer fence or begin the beautiful wall. Maybe the Republicans simply do not like Donald Trump. Yet, when they refuse to do their jobs well, they hurt the American people. Bannon and Hannon finish their expose on Ryan with the following:

*"Yet Ryan's omnibus serves a second and equally chilling purpose. By locking in the President's refugee, immigration, and spending priorities, Ryan's bill is designed to keep these fights out of Congress by getting them off the table for good. Delivering Obama these wins– and pushing these issues beyond the purview of Congress–will suppress public attention to the issues and, in so doing, will boost the candidacy of the Republican establishment's preferred presidential contenders, who favor President Obama's immigration agenda."*

*"What may prove most discouraging of all to Americans is that recent reports reveal that conservatives in the so-called House Freedom Caucus are praising Ryan even as he permanently locks in*

*these irreversible and anti-American immigration policies. According to Politico, the House Freedom Caucus will "give Ryan a pass" even as he funds disastrous policies that prioritize the interests of foreign nationals and global corporatists above the needs of the American people, whom lawmakers are supposed to represent."*

Mick Jagger would say that "You can't always get what you want." This is a far cry from promising one thing and doing exactly the opposite. Question: Why do Republican elites continue to lie? Answer: Because we let them. Even with their lies, they appear to be the better choice rather than electing leftist Democrats.

That is, the Republicans *appeared* to be the better choice until the notion of The John Doe Party was introduced. Now, if only we could find some folks with some spare change who are willing and able to donate and help coordinate the efforts to create a John Doe Party.

Just as the Republican Party once took on the Whig party and won; then one term later got its first President in Abraham Lincoln, we could do it with the right organization and the right team. But first we must believe we can. Back when the Republicans got a foothold in the 1850's, there was no Internet to get the word out quickly. We should be able to get it done today with less effort! Let's go do it!

Hey Buddy, can you spare a dime?

# Chapter 6    Democrats, Republicans, and Party Elites?

## Are party labels meaningful?

I am a registered Democrat. More and more of my Democrat friends are switching to Republican or Independent to get away from the leftist. socialist, progressive and communist viewpoints of the Democrat Party leaders. I heard another today say "I did not leave the Democratic Party. The Party left me." I am a white male and I know that does not put me in good standing with the Democrat leadership. I ran for office a few times and not a soul from the Democratic party contacted me. Was it because I am white; because I am anti-leftist or because I think people should not depend on government. Probably it was all of the above.

I thought a number of times about becoming a Republican. Though the Republicans do not lie as regularly as the Democrats, with McConnell and Ryan running things, you can no longer trust them as far as you can throw them. This book is loaded with examples of Republican betrayals. And, so I am now a big advocate for the creation of The John Doe Party and I would be pleased to be its second member after we find ourselves a founding donor who is also a regular American.

Americans need no more evidence that party labels are largely meaningless than what is happening right in front of them. Who is listening to the people? No political party is listening and no party is hearing the people of America. Democrat leadership refuses to use its ears. And, of course the newly "bipartisan" ruling establishment; influential members of the establishment wing of the GOP — neocons, warmongers, globalists, and so on hear nothing if it does not benefit them personally. What difference does a label make when opinions are already formed?

With Donald Trump as our President, thinking Americans are very happy and could not be happier with our chief executive. Unfortunately, even with President Trump in charge of the Executive Branch, all is not well in America. If this were not America, a wise guy would likely say that something is rotten in the State of Denmark. But, this is America, and yes, something is rotten in the American 50 states. We have half of the Republicans and all of the Democrats trying to undermine the duly elected President of the United States. Many anti-leftist American John Does would like to see them arrested for Treason.

There is a cadre of miscreants who are part of the Republican Elite Establishment with some beholden to big donors and K-street lobbyists. In the recent presidential election, these Republicans showed their true colors and the real allegiances they have kept hidden over the years.

Regular Americans, populists, and nationalists, who had often looked to the Republican Party for values and overall goodness, even after many broken promises, have been somewhat surprised to find the Republican establishment elites choosing self-interests over American interests. The game has not changed much but today, Republicans are bold enough to their politics in the open.

From the Bush war hawks who pushed Americans into war; to pretend conservatives; to the globalist hot shot members of the Council on Foreign Relations—even those like me from other Parties, looking for leadership from the Republican Party, have found a void, and have concluded rightfully that there is nothing to find.

There once were the Republicans in Name Only (RINOs) siding with Democrats against the American people. In the presidential election, they were emboldened enough to point blank offer that they were planning to vote for Hillary Clinton at a time when she appeared to be a viable candidate. I am sure they voted for her but of course, she was not viable and she lost big.

These Republican traitors had no problem proclaiming that the Republican candidate Donald Trump was unfit to serve. Now, he is their President but they seem not to have accepted him. They are learning that actively being against Trump may not serve them and their selfish wants and needs in the future but it is not yet inhibiting them.

Many of us who know them too well, still can envision the pomposity of these globalist RINOs and neocon warmongers as they were nestled in comfortable, well-padded seats, sipping their sweet Pina Coladas in the bar-cars on the Hillary Train.

Just take a look for a minute at the massive history book *Tragedy and Hope*, written by Bill Clinton mentor and establishment insider Carroll Quigley. In it, Quigley explains as succinctly and as pithily as can be, how American politics actually works in the real world. The real world is where those, whose incomes do not come close to millions per year, live and work. It is also the world in which the elite establishment believe their rule over political matters is absolute.

Quigley also explains that the benefits for those living outside the working-class confines are so great for the elite that these insiders absolutely love it and simply do not care, nor have they really ever cared which party wins elections as long as they are members of the club of all important members, not associated with the common folk.

"The argument that the two parties should represent opposed ideals and policies, one, perhaps, of the Right and the other of the Left, is a foolish idea acceptable only to doctrinaire and academic thinkers,"

Quigley offers his conclusions with no emotion though it is huge news to most hoi polloi activists in both parties. He offers his own version of Nirvana: "Instead, the two parties should be almost identical, so that the American people can 'throw the rascals out' at any election without leading to any profound or extensive shifts in policy."

This explains why for so long and even now that he is President, so many "important" Republicans seem to hate Donald Trump in so many unexplained ways. As far as the elitists in the establishment are concerned, Trump is still a danger to their status as globalists which they have been enjoying.

Trump, with full support of real Americans who love America proudly, during the campaign slammed the Hillary-backed Iraq and Libyan wars and he blasted "globalism" as a threat to the interests of all Americans. Meanwhile Trump himself as President has emerged as the biggest threat to that whole "uniparty" idea. And, here I am talking about a movement to The John Doe Party. Now we're talking!

There was a time when I thought that Rush Limbaugh had all the answers. Well, I think he has most answers but on the rationale for why the Republicans were falling off the Party Bandwagon, abandoning Trump in record numbers I had not heard Quigley's notion from Rush Limbaugh as of today.

Yet, the smartest guy on why Trump has no big-time Republican player support. It now seems to be Alex Neuman, who is smart enough to quote a lot of Quigley when he offers his thoughts on the issue. I'd like to see what Rush Limbaugh thinks about this characterization!

Neuman hit a home run in his July 28, 2016 piece on thenewamerican.com web site. It is titled: "Neocons, *Warmongers, and Globalists Abandon GOP for Hillary.* It explains it all and it is a pretty disgusting thought for any American who wants America to continue to be America. Thankfully the election is over and Trump is our President. Now, these Neocons, Warmongers, and Globalists seem to be doing whatever they can to destroy the Trump presidency.

Neuman and Quigley immediately answer the question that anti-leftist regular Americans have had since Republicans gained back the power in the House: "Why is nobody doing anything to stop Obama?" We have called Republicans names such as Wimps and RINOS and other unflattering terms as we watched them give it all up for Obama. After offering no fight, the RINOS gave the President all the budget money he needed to destroy our way of life. Quigley nailed it and Neuman blasts it out of the park with impunity.

The Republicans who run the Party do not care at all about the Party or the country. They do care about being cronies, warmongers, neocons, and globalists rather than being Americans. That's it. If America no longer offers them the big-ticket items at a deal because of Trump, they will stay switched to Democrat, as many have already done! That is how much these self-indulgent traitors care about having it their way.

It seems that the free press is bought and paid for by the Democratic Party and thus it is not really free and thus it no longer serves as the fourth estate. It cannot be trusted under any circumstances.

Every now and then the press may get it right but by accident. My great friend Dennis Grimes loves to say, "Even a blind squirrel finds a nut once in a while." A recent theorem by Rush Limbaugh posits that the ownership role of the press may be reversed. He thinks that the press has become its own Political Party and it is the Press that controls the Democratic party rather than vice versa. Interesting.

Before the election Neuman wrote:

"Ironically, establishment media outlets are touting the establishment GOP defections to Hillary among neocons and globalists in an apparent effort to hurt the Trump campaign. Apparently, they are oblivious to the fact that the defections of widely loathed establishment warmongers from Republican ranks actually bolsters Trump's arguments of a "rigged" system — not to mention his credibility in the eyes of supporters on both sides of the political spectrum, including among embattled "working class voters" and union members long considered reliable Democrats...

Thank you Mr. Neuman

Why were so many big shots breaking off the Republican bandwagon in the light of day? First of all; it is because they thought it was safe to do so. They don't see themselves getting hurt because a good number of their cronies were doing the same thing. It was also because they have always been self-first and when Trump threatened their comfortable way of life, by planning to drain the swamp, they found jumping the Republican ship as a way to protect themselves

The biggest mass exodus from anything that anybody saw during the election and to today however, is the exodus of pure conservatives from being just conservatives to becoming populists and nationalists. In fact,

Trump opened a lot of eyes. Many, including Rush Limbaugh no longer use the conservative moniker but instead call themselves anti-leftists which also helps them segregate themselves from RINO and Establishment anti-Trump Republicans.

Donald Trump has taught us all that what has really been aggravating us about the stodgy elitists in the GOP, especially recently, is that we are Americans for America, and they are selfish louts out for themselves. We had never gotten the message that patriotism was dead.

Trump has revived patriotism so much that supporters, even when they are upset at some of Trump's positions, are tickled pink that Donald Trump is President. Nobody else has the charisma and the inner toughness to work so hard for the American people in such a difficult role.

We the people see Trump's presidential campaign and his election and now his governance as the birth of a new American right, that is built on a strong desire to feel good again about America. It is based upon a sense of nationalism and populism that has always been there but may have been buried somewhere in our conservatism.

No longer are conservatives fully ideologically pure, and that is OK because nobody of whom I am aware at the grassroots level, where I live, is moving from conservative to liberal or progressive or Marxist. We are looking for goodness in leadership to bring us a great future. We are thankful that Donald Trump is that leader!

I listen to Limbaugh every day for three hours, except for the time from 12 to 3 that I doze off as it is nap time for all sixty-nine-year-olds. Nationalism and populism have clearly overtaken conservatism in terms of appeal," Limbaugh has been saying this quite often recently. He is right on the mark. Anti-leftist is also right on the mark.

Rush Limbaugh well understands that many voters are simply "fed up" with the Democratic Party and have been for quite a while. They had been patient with Republicans for years but saw no action coupled with a new and obvious disdain for the anti-left masses. And, so now, we the people have become angry with Republicans in Congress, and we simply no longer trust them with our political fate.

We are angry with those who provide no real opposition in Washington. Who is supposed to take on the Democrats if not Republicans? Thankfully, the actions of elitist establishment Republicans did not mean that we got Hillary for eight years after Obama. Isn't that great?

We the unwashed masses are the new-nationalists and populists while we are still mostly conservative and all-anti-leftist. We are taken up with the idea that we might be able to fall in love with Al Jolson's America again along with Frank Capra's America as we can play his old songs and watch Capra's movies in a happier America. You see, with Trump, it is not pure conservatism that has united us or has motivated us. It is America.

Until Trump came along, none of us were really sure. That's what everybody had been missing in Washington and throughout the country. American conservatives have found a way to bring back our America and it is not by being staunch Republicans. It is by following Donald Trump now that he is President and winning the day for America and Americans.

We saw Obama as the anti-American and Hillary as the same. That is why so many John Does came out to assure America did not get eight more years of anti-American policies with Hillary. Donald Trump is our Captain America. He is a phenomenon and history will record him as such. My friends and I are very glad he was in the race and we ae elated that he won the race. Bravo President Trump!

We wish that he is careful as he engages the swamp as the swamp dwellers will do their best to hurt him if he chooses to trust them. Donald Trump, I predict, would switch to the John Doe Party if it were available for him. Hopefully, the rest of the Trump family will help with the movement to John Doe Clubs and ultimately The John Doe Party.

Everything that Obama and Hillary stand for, we have been against and continue to be against. It is axiomatic. We are in direct opposition to the left, to the Democratic Party, to Obama, to Hillary, to the leftist press, and everything that has been going on for the last eight years. We are still mad as hell and we want it all stopped and reversed. The right guy is in charge. That man is a unique truth-teller in an era of lies. That man is Donald Trump.  Would it not be great if four years from now, Donald Trump were President of the United States, after being nominated from the thick of The John Doe Party Convention.

We like Trump as much for the fact that we do not perceive him as part of the establishment as we do for his simple solutions that are best for America. Even if the solutions are difficult to achieve, we admire Donald Trump for having the moxie to get on the ball-field and do his best to win the game. We believe in his ability to make us all winners. There will be no losses and no losers on the Trump team. And, we will never get sick of winning.

Rush Limbaugh knows that Americans are angry at "Republican establishment central" in Washington. Donald Trump shares our anger and disdain for *Establishment Central*, and we love him for that.

Limbaugh believes that the new Nationalists and Populists are not necessarily committed as much to the conservative orthodoxy, especially when it comes to abstract principles or free market economics. For me, I have always been America-first but nobody other than Donald Trump has capitalized on that notion. And so, as a regular John Doe American, I have no problem being a Nationalist and a Populist. I want America to survive and have a great future.

"They don't have to be conservative," Trump explained. "They don't even have to be Republican." As a Democrat myself, I found that refreshing. I am a future John Doe man.

On a recent show, Limbaugh read from a 1996 article in the magazine Chronicles titled "From Household to Nation," authored by the late Sam Francis.

He was discussing populism and nationalism when he quoted Sam Francis from this 1996 article. Here is the quote:

"Sooner or later, as the globalist elites seek to drag the country into conflicts and global commitments, preside over the economic pastoralization of the United States, manage the delegitimization of our own culture, and the dispossession of our people, and disregard or diminish our national interests and national sovereignty, a nationalist reaction is almost inevitable and will probably assume populist form when it arrives."

When Francis was writing this piece in 1996, he was talking about a rogue Patrick Buchanan presidential campaign. Francis had served as an adviser to the campaign. Ironically, though Buchanan is unquestionably one of America's great ones, Francis's prognostication can be brought into the present and just about all he wrote applies to Donald Trump. One can see in Francis's writings that he was predicting the rise of Trump.

We all know that Trump's signature issues are opposition to illegal immigration and opposition to bad trade deals against American interests. Trump is not just a man that gets our nationalist pro-American juices going, he has the ideas necessary to do the right thing even though the donor class—the real leaders and financiers of the swamp, is against it.

That is why so many of the establishment elites are against Donald Trump and why the people who learned who he is were so dedicated to his victory. Government hates him. Elitist establishment Democrats and Republicans hate him. Union bosses hate him yet their members love him. Corporations hate him, and of course the corrupt media, a branch of the Democratic Party or vice versa also hate Trump. Only real people—my neighbors and your neighbors like Trump because he is hell-bent on creating an America for us, not for the donor class to count their increasing wealth,

That means CNN. MSNBC, ABC, NBC, and CBS all hate Trump and unfortunately for conservatives, half of the bigshots on Fox openly hate trump. Again, that is a big reason why the people love him. Those guys that we love to hate; hate Trump.

In days' past, even the Robber Barons cared about America, while they cared about their wealth. They were not at odds with the country. Today it seems our culture has given the big and the powerful the right to enjoy their riches selfishly and not to worry about anybody or anything else—even their country.

Today as I was at Mass, I heard a great homily. The Priest talked about rich people who love their money more than anything else. It made me think of the elite establishment in both political parties. No time to worry about anybody else while collecting all their gains and fixing elections with their available cash.

## Bury your heat with your riches

St. Anthony of Padua has a big heart and in one of his sermons at the death bed of a rich man, he suggested that the dead man's remains had everything but a heart. His heart was not with the poor or the needy or with those he should have loved, but instead, Anthony told the crowd at the funeral that this man's heart was buried with his treasure, and it was not with his body. He asked the participants in the funeral to go ahead and see for themselves. This is that story:

"In a few words, on true and false love, [St. Anthony] preached at the funeral of the Florentine notable! Anthony's text was: "Where thy treasure is there thy heart is also." Pausing suddenly, he beheld in a vision the soul of that rich man in torment. He exclaimed: "This rich man is dead and his soul is in torture! Go open his coffers and you will find his heart." The astonished relatives and friends hastened to do his bidding; and there, half buried among the gold pieces, they found the still palpitating heart of the dead Croesus."

The good news today is that a billionaire such as Donald Trump with a heart and with a lot of love for family, friends and country chose to serve America. His heart will not be with his coffers, We the people need Donald Trump more than he needs us. He is one of a kind. Now that we elected him, let's help him get the job done in whatever way we can. Speak up when somebody defames America by defaming our President.

Big time billionaire Meg Whitman, who has been trying to win elections as a Republican for years, but nobody wants her, is currently the CEO of HP. Maybe she bought her way into the job. All I know is she has no loyalty to HP or to her Party, the Republican Party. She made the news before the election for abandoning the Republican Party because of its support for Donald Trump. Whitman changed to the "D." Party. Good riddens! Great! I hope she stays there unless she recants.

She went all out for Hillary Clinton. She donated as much as she could to Hillary. Of course, Whitman knew that when Trump, a man for the people was elected, her wealth would not increase. But, if Hillary, a broker for the status quo in which rich Meg could get richer, while regular Americans stagnated, were elected President, then Whitman's heart would be surrounded by lots more gold and treasures in her coffers. Like the dead Croesus, her misplaced heart could beat for eternity, separated by her body and soul. Perhaps Donald Trump saved Meg Whitman from such an eternity. I hope so, but she should recant.

Talking about a traitor. But, maybe not! Maybe Whitman never, ever, was a conservative. When trying to be elected, maybe she was faking us all; maybe she would have kept up the fake and she might have tried to run again for Republican President if she did not think Trump was going to win this time.

Donald Trump, in his own unique way brought out the truth in a lot of stodgy old billionaires, male and female, such as Meg Whitman, along with big-time "R" donors, who demand their pound of flesh from America.

We won't be seeing any of them in the American Legion or in the VFW any time soon anyway, as they stay clear of the great unwashed masses of John Doe Americans. But, I think we will begin to see a great guy like Donald Trump—a real American—at American Legions and VFW's and VA Hospitals across the land. Don't you think? Where will you find Meg Whitman? Look up the word, "posh."

A caller on the Rush Limbaugh show this past week put the Meg Whitman deal in perspective. As CEO of HP, she cares about corporate profits before she has any thoughts on America and Americans. The caller discussed what he called a secret policy at HP that was to assure 70% of American jobs with HP would be gone.

The jobs would be offshored so the corporation could make more money. That sounds like Meg Whitman. So, one would think that in addition to union workers, the corporate employees and retirees who learn about their company CEOs being anti-Trump, will become Trump guys like many of us. He has an anti-off-shoring stance. No regular American who worked for an offshoring type of corporation, ever begged the corporation to ship out even more jobs. These folks will be pressed to vote for Trump to protect American jobs.

We all know some big names like the three Bushes, Romney, Whitman, and others who are still on the *Never Trump* bandwagon. I wondered before the election who they expected to appoint the next Supreme Court Nominees—Hillary Rodham Clinton? Let's remember these names listed below and remember that they let us all down by playing for the other team. Do not elect them for dogcatcher and if you can buy a product from another company than from one, whose CEO is against Trump, please do so.

A list of others, traitorous Republicans, who have disgraced their own Party and who have abandoned their nominee, Donald Trump, who may or may not be on the list of disgraced "Republican" neocons, globalists, and establishment insiders but who fully pushed a Clinton presidency, include the following names. Don't ever forget them!"

- ✓ Ken Adelman
- ✓ Rep. Justin Amash, R-Mich.
- ✓ Richard Armitage
- ✓ Gov. Charlie Baker, R-Mass.
- ✓ Brian Bartlett (Romney)
- ✓ Glenn Beck
- ✓ Michael Berry
- ✓ Max Boot (Rubio)
- ✓ George Bush the Elder
- ✓ George W. Bush
- ✓ Jeb Bush

- ✓ Sally Bradshaw
- ✓ Bruce Carroll,
- ✓ Jay Caruso, RedState
- ✓ Mona Charen,
- ✓ Linda Chavez
- ✓ Dean Clancy
- ✓ Eliot Cohen (Bush)
- ✓ Sen. Norm Coleman, R-Minn.
- ✓ Maria Comella
- ✓ Charles C. W. Cooke
- ✓ Doug Coon
- ✓ Rory Cooper
- ✓ Jim Cunneen
- ✓ Rep. Carlos Curbelo, R-Fla.
- ✓ Steve Deace
- ✓ Rep. Bob Dold, R-Ill.
- ✓ Erick Erickson
- ✓ Mindy Finn
- ✓ Tony Fratto
- ✓ David French
- ✓ Jon Gabriel
- ✓ Sen. Lindsey Graham, R-S.C.
- ✓ Michael Graham
- ✓ Jonah Goldberg
- ✓ Alan Goldsmith
- ✓ Stephen Gutowski
- ✓ Rep. Richard Hanna, R-N.Y
- ✓ Jamie Brown Hantman
- ✓ Stephen Hayes,
- ✓ Doug Heye
- ✓ Quin Hillyer
- ✓ Ben Howe,
- ✓ Brit Hume (Fox)
- ✓ Rep. Bob Inglis, R-S.C.
- ✓ Cheri Jacobus
- ✓ Robert Kagan
- ✓ John Kasich
- ✓ Randy Kendrick (big donor)
- ✓ Matt Kibbe

- ✓ Rep. Adam Kinzinger, R-Ill.
- ✓ Philip Klein
- ✓ Charles Krauthamme (Fox)
- ✓ Bill Kristol
- ✓ Mark Levin
- ✓ Justin LoFranco (Walker)
- ✓ Kevin Madden (Romney)
- ✓ Bethany Mandel
- ✓ Tucker Martin
- ✓ Gov. Bob McDonnell's, R-Va.
- ✓ Mel Martínez (RNC)
- ✓ Liz Mair
- ✓ Lachlan Markey
- ✓ David McIntosh
- ✓ Dan McLaughlin
- ✓ Ken Mehlman (RNC)
- ✓ Tim Miller
- ✓ Joyce Mulliken
- ✓ Ted Newton (Romney)
- ✓ James Nuzzo
- ✓ Katie Packer
- ✓ Gov. George Pataki, R-N.Y.
- ✓ Henry "Hank" Paulson
- ✓ Rep. Ron Paul, R-Texas
- ✓ Katie Pavlich
- ✓ Brittany Pounders
- ✓ Rep. Reid Ribble, R- Wisc.
- ✓ Ricketts family, (GOP mega-donors)
- ✓ Gov. Tom Ridge, R-Pa.
- ✓ Rep. Scott Rigell, R-Va.
- ✓ Mitt Romney
- ✓ Paul Rosenzweig
- ✓ Karl Rove
- ✓ Jennifer Rubin
- ✓ Patrick Ruffini
- ✓ Sarah Rumpf
- ✓ Mark Salter
- ✓ Rep. Mark Sanford, R-S.C.
- ✓ Sen. Ben Sasse, R- Neb.

- ✓ Elliott Schwartz
- ✓ Gabriel Schoenfeld
- ✓ Tara Setmayer
- ✓ Ben Shapiro,
- ✓ Evan Siegfried
- ✓ Ben Stein
- ✓ Alan Steinberg
- ✓ Brendan Steinhauser
- ✓ Stuart Stevens (Romney)
- ✓ Paul Singer (GOP donor)
- ✓ Erik Soderstrom (Fiorina)
- ✓ Charlie Sykes
- ✓ Brad Thor
- ✓ Senator Pat Toomey (R-PA)
- ✓ Michael R. Treiser (Romney)
- ✓ Daniel P. Vajdich (Cruz)
- ✓ Connor Walsh (Cantor)
- ✓ Rep. J.C. Watts, R-Okla.
- ✓ Peter Wehner
- ✓ Gov. Christine Todd Whitman, R-N.J.
- ✓ Meg Whitman (HP)
- ✓ George Will,
- ✓ Rick Wilson, Nathan Wurtzel
- ✓ Bill Yarbrough
- ✓ Dave Yost

That's not all and there will be more. Use the list above as your own personal starter set and add names as you learn about them. Washington insiders, aka the swamp, are threatened that Donald Trump, one of the few good guys out there may take the gravy train right from their mouths.

These people are lobbyists or are taking the money of lobbyists to undermine the American people. It actually proves Trump's point that he was the non-establishment candidate. He is an American for America and those traitor Republicans are why he well deserved his election victory. I would be disappointed if they liked him.

The good news for America is that another fifty came out of hiding on August 8, 2016 just in time to help Trump get a bounce from his great economic speech.  Yes, fifty prominent Republican foreign policy and national security experts -- many veterans of George W. Bush's administration—aka elite establishment Republicans signed a letter denouncing Donald Trump's presidential candidacy and they pledged not to vote for him. The people overrode their disdain for Trump and voted him in as President. These fifty are simply traitors and they still think they own the Republican Party. Well, their money will not buy the people anymore.

The letter they wrote includes the ultimate slam: "We are convinced that in the Oval Office, he would be the most reckless President in American history." These are all Bushies and because Jeb got his poor little feelings hurt when he spent over $100 million and Trump had spent nothing and Jeb could not get more than 5% of the vote, he had to blame somebody. So, he blamed Trump, the guy who beat him.

Now, the Jeb Bush loyalists—all elite Republicans and members of clubs, which have policies to keep you and I from ever getting close to their parking lots, hoping to protect their lobbyist cash, tried to fool Americans by attempting to sully Trump's reputation. Good luck. Most Americans do not like cry-babies.

By the way, my personal thanks to these 50, Thanks for coming out of hiding as anti-Republican. You people are why Republicans lose elections. You are all worthless traitors who found more value in Hillary Clinton than the man Republican voters chose as the nominee of the people -- what was once your Party. Then, we voted him in as our President.

Besides the group listed above, you know who you are. Your names are on that nasty letter. I am talking about all those Bushie sycophants who had been dependent on the Bush machine over the years including former CIA and National Security Agency Director Michael Hayden, former Director of National Intelligence and Deputy Secretary of State John Negroponte and Eric Edelman, who was Vice President Dick Cheney's national security adviser and has worked closely with Michele Flournoy -- a candidate for secretary of defense in a prospective Clinton administration -- to forge a centrist group of defense experts on key military issues.

Doesn't President Trump look great as he was becoming our President

The list of traitors kept growing and still is growing as others come out of hiding. The announced traitors in this next batch included two Homeland Security secretaries under Bush, Tom Ridge and Michael Chertoff, and Robert Zoellick, a former World Bank president, U.S. trade representative and deputy secretary of state. These guys are such big shots, the doors in their homes had to be widened just to help get their big heads in. Trump's campaign at the time responded appropriately to the traitors with a statement from Trump denouncing the signatories as the very people who deserve the "blame for making the world such a dangerous place." Amen!

When Republican non-elites (folks like you and I) have the great sense to no longer cling to a party that has abandoned them, this new notion of which I speak, The John Doe Party will save our day. Meanwhile, those Republicans who chose to abandon their Party, with a partial list shown above, will rue the day. Why would one of us ever give them an opportunity for anything in the future after that have plotted and almost destroyed our county?

God Bless America a million zillion times. We all need it!

# Chapter 7   Wimpy Republicans Killed the Party

## The 2017 party of wimps

Let the Republican leadership and the elitist conservatives in the shadows stand down.

Though Democrats, my dad and I, well before he died, began seeing the Democrats as anti-American and the Republicans as a Party offering great hope for America. That is the way it was. The more I learned about the Republican Party at first the more I liked them. How could you not like Ronald Reagan? So, I wanted them to do as much for America as possible. I knew Dems would do nothing right. After Reagan, however, the more I was disappointed as the Republicans consistently seemed to be a party of cannot, rather than can. The party mantra was to be able to snatch defeat from the jaws of victory, knowingly or unknowingly.

Of course, I was not quite as politically astute then so when I finally noticed the new Republicans, among other things, I started trying to figure out just how long the party of Lincoln, the Grand Old Party—had been playing lap dog for the Democrats?  I remember many disappointments over the years. So, for Democrats, as a Democrat I developed a disgust in the pit of my stomach, and for Republicans I was continually disappointed.  What was left?

I am sure it is more than twenty years ago and probably more than thirty that this phenomenon began. Conservatives have been far too patient, rooting for a Party that no longer has respect for even itself.

You probably did not believe how many conservatives had become upset with Republicans, and you probably did not believe how many use the same exact term—"wimps," to describe the Republicans of today. Then, along came Trump, just as in the 1950's when the song "Along Came Jones" was determined to make everything right again. You may know that this fabulous song, Along Came Jones was recorded on March 26, 1959 by the Coasters and released in May 1959. They sure were great days in America. Back then, fun was permitted and free speech was taken for granted. I going to use a smidgeon of free speech right here to say that I am really tickled that I can sing a song with the same melody today with the title, Along Came Trump. After the last eight years, it is a thrill to sing a positive song. about America.

Wimp is the right word for the elitist Republicans of today for sure. For those doubters, here is a definition for WIMP:

*a weak and cowardly or unadventurous person.*

Yes sir! We sure have picked the right word. Indeed! Well, since most of you reading this book are anti-leftists or conservatives, I suspect you believe it and you are not surprised.

I hope you enjoy the beginning of this article from 1994 titled, "Wimpy Republicans." It is nice to have our conclusions affirmed and this article does that and more. If we substituted the gang of eight amnesty charade or the Mayday 2017 Omnibus bill for the crime bill in this article, it would sound like it was written quite recently.

## "Wimpy Republicans" September 09, 1994 by Mona Charen from the Baltimore Sun

"THE CAPITULATION of six frightened, feeble, supine Republican senators on the so-called crime bill does not bode well for the debate over [Hillary's] health care legislation. It suggests that some Republicans are still playing by rules invented by and for Democrats. If those rules are followed on health, we will get some kind of reform bill -- and that will be terrible for the country and politically damaging for Republicans as well.

"The rules that were followed on the crime bill are as follows: The Democrats propose a huge federal spending program to address a problem that ought not to be handled by the federal government in the first place. The Republicans complain about the cost. The Democrats accuse the Republicans of being "anti-elderly" or "anti-children." Republicans stammer in response. The Democrats make some minor adjustments to the act (like cutting $3 billion from the $33 billion crime bill), and the Republicans vote for it."

The more things change, the more they stay the same. I found the scenario similar to today and utterly amazing that this has been going on for so long that few can remember when Republican leaders had any guts.

On December 11, 2011, Republicans were at it again. Here is a part of a piece from conservativeviewsforthegrassroots.com:

*"Republicans caved under pressure. ... though a two-month extension won't solve things in the long term, it will help temporarily to give the 2 million people out of work some reprieve and spare doctors from a big Medicare cut. This will save each tax payer $40 per paycheck. This is called deferring the battle for another day. In other words, Congress is being stupid. A two-month extension only perpetuates the uncertainty that too many employers already have in dealing with the economy and what's coming out of Washington. Prolonging the agony will not suffice the American people."*

Conservatives have been begging Republicans to do their jobs for an awful long time. Republican leadership with orders from the Donor class and the K-Street swamp, have quietly refused. Now that Donald Trump and the people demand that they do their jobs, they find it more convenient to attack Donald Trump and the people.

On May 7, 2013, in Virginia, the **state** Republicans chose to emulate Capitol Hill. This excerpt is from beforeitsnews.com:

*"Remember that commercial for trash-bags; the one that describes their competitors trash-bags as wimpy, wimpy, wimpy. When I see other states and their reaction to the Federal government on the 2nd Amendment and other issues; that "wimpy, wimpy, wimpy" phrase perfectly describes your GOP legislators in Virginia.*

*Bob Marshall's exceptionally weak 2nd Amendment protection bill couldn't even make it out of a committee as GOP lawmakers wrung their hands that they might offend their "friends" in Washington. While Virginia Republicans cower, and shake, other states are standing up for their citizens' rights."*

On December 3, 2012, Michael Reagan made some astute observations about the GOP:

*"Republicans had better learn from history -- and from Ronald Reagan's mistake.*

*President Obama and his fellow big-spenders in Congress are promising if they get higher tax rates today they'll make even higher spending cuts tomorrow.*

*It's an old sucker's game. Republicans -- and the rest of the country -- should know it by now, because for three decades we've all been suckers.*

*If history is our guide, and Republicans in Congress don't grow a spine, by this time next year we'll have higher taxes, higher spending, more debt and a bigger government."*

Republicans have not only become wimpy on conservative issues, fiscal, social, and moral; they are also stupid, looking to Democrats for their next move.  The bottom line on why it is time for conservatives to get it going ourselves comes from Douglas MacKinnon in late spring 2013. His article for Townhall.com is very compelling. Too bad it is so true.

*"If you are a conservative and someone who believes in the foundation of traditional values, then it's time to face a sad truth -- the Republican Party of 2013 and still in 2017 is all but useless to you."*

*"Be it the current and exponentially growing scandals of Benghazi, the IRS deliberately targeting conservative groups, or the Obama administration trying to intimidate -- and potentially jail -- certain members of the media, or the immigration "debate," one thing is all but certain: The Republican "leadership" and its lieutenants will eventually roll over and look the other way." Mayday 2017 was another roll-over.*

Until Trump came along and these leaders quickly joined the "Never Trumpers." most Americans did not know that elitist establishment Republicans were against the people—even conservative people. Right before the election, these same wimps were joining the Democratic Party and singing loud: "Heil Hillary!"

And, so I am using this forum to add my voice to the long chorus of conservatives (aka anti-leftists) who are fed up being victimized by the Republican Party. We need to have the courage to change the elitist candidate and the Party itself if Republican leadership will not.

We were fortunate enough this time to get our candidate, Trump. Now that he elected, with minimal help from the Republican Establishment, we now need to work on either changing the Party, changing its name, or better yet, killing the Republican Party and going with a better reflection of America – The John Doe party.

## The John Doe Party needs a well-monied regular American to help establish this new party!

When I first conceived of the notion of this book, I was hoping that I could get a great conservative (anti-leftist) spokesperson, such as Rush Limbaugh or Michelle Malkin, or Laura Ingraham to co-author it. I thought of Mark Steyn and Mark Levyn also but my attempts to contact any of these stalwart conservatives were futile. Despite my 115 prior books, they still don't know me.

I suspect they all have their hotlines so they can communicate among each other but, no matter what I tried, I could not get a nibble.  Now, I regret to say that Mark Levyn started out for Hillary because he hated Trump so much. Levyn, who I always admired, is a smart guy and he finally realized that Trump was not the problem, but the solution. Now, Mark Levyn is in the Trump camp. Thank the Lord!

So, here I am again, a voice crying out in the desert, hoping to be heard by anti-leftist conservatives so that together we can change the end of America from something that must be to something that might be. The Republicans are playing the part of Scrooge, but Dickens may very well have written a few different endings. My advice to anti-leftists, conservatives, and nationalists is that we can no longer count on Republicans to fight our battles for the values which we hold dear. Donald Trump has yet to have a problem handling most of our load, and he is strong enough to make and keep America strong. We are lucky indeed. Viva El Presidente!

I am especially pleased that my local paper published a short letter to the editor that I submitted to their mailbag in 2013. In it as you will see, I publicly asked some of these same prominent conservatives for their help with this book. As the Beatles wrote, "No Reply." I saw the light but nobody came forth. I did not really expect that they would hear about this piece in the Times Leader from Wilkes-Barre PA, but "Hope springs eternal."

This is the article I wrote that was published by the Times Leader in Wilkes-Barre PA on Sunday August 4, 2013.

The book referenced below has been published and has already been met with success.

Amazon.com/author/brianwkelly

This is not that book. It is similar in that it points out the problems with trusting Republicans. Substitute the John Doe Party for American Party below and the message is very similar.

# Replace the GOP with Americans

*"I am working on a new book that I plan to title, Kill the Republican Party. (Subsequently there was an alternate renaming to Bring on the American Party, [which did not stick] I would love to get a great spokesman of conservatism such as Rush Limbaugh or Michelle Malkin, to co-author it but so far, they are too busy with their shows and premium subscribers to respond to my many inquiries. Maybe eventually, they will hear my entreaties and help the American cause. [Call in when you have a chance and ask them to add to the follow-up, or perhaps a reprint.]*

*The book is about how the Republicans have chosen to abandon conservative Americans so they can become the ME-TOO Democrat Party and possibly trick some otherwise fine conservatives into thinking that conservatives have a bad message for the country. We don't!*

*Unfortunately, Republicans do not believe they need conservatives any more in their Party. They know we do not agree with them while they choose to lean towards the same progressive agenda as our most un-trusted liberal friends. They think we do not matter. We matter more than anybody thinks!*

*Don't you think that we Libertarians and Republican conservatives and even folks like me, who are bona fide conservative Democrats should be able to join together to form something to replace the anachronistic Republican Party?*

*It should be the American Party since the Republicans and the Democrats have chosen to unite to become fully self-serving in their treatment of the American public. Neither the Democrats nor the Republicans in Congress care about regular Americans... Democrat and Republican lawmakers are simply corrupt. They both choose to trick Americans into thinking they are on our side. They are not on our side...*

*Democrats of yesterday (not their leadership) are now conservatives. Today's takers from the treasury are now Democrats. Today's conservatives that think they are Republicans are reminded every day that the real Republicans do not want conservative Americans in their ranks.*

*Years ago, I defined a Republican as somebody with over $50 million in the bank. Maybe it is more. I think if the conservatives without $50 million in the bank left the Republican Party and formed the American Party, this would be a bullet that would decimate the Republican Party. The negative consequences of the Party's death are greatly exaggerated. Let them swallow their wealth.*

*The American Party can become a party to embrace real Americans. Let the Republicans and Democrats swim in their own brine of corruption.*
"

*Signed, Brian Kelly*

This Book, "It's Time for the John Doe Party," is a grown-up version of Kill the Republican Party – Bring on the American Party. How many times must regular John Does be kicked in the teeth by "well-meaning" Republicans to realize that does not help. Regular John Does in America need The John Doe Party to bring the Republic back to the people.

Well, you can see in my published letter to the editor that I had to get that off my chest. I now know that regular Americans know how I stand. Don't all anti-leftist conservatives feel as I do? Don't you wish that elite establishment Republicans who still have great American values could regain control of the party from those we call either RINOs or Republican wimps?

It does not seem likely, however. It appears the best solution is to bring forth The John Doe Party as suggested in this book and all anti leftists would then choose to exit the Republican Party gracefully.

Additionally, anti-leftist Democrats would be welcomed immediately. Having a John Doe Party is all the more possible now that Donald J. Trump has been elected President of the United States of America. Wouldn't he make a great first president for the John Doe Party?

## Republicans chose to abandon conservatives

In this past election in which Donald Trump became our President, a lot of big shot Republicans have chosen to abandon anti-leftist conservative Americans so they could become part of the ME-TOO Democrat Party. My Republican brother Joe calls his new party, Democrat-Lite and he is not happy at all about the change.

Joe was not asked about the platform going liberal progressive. I suspect that many Americans feel the same. It is very proper to call each and every one of the new Republican leaders, RINOS. I am so pleased that Trump took it to them all in the 2016 Republican Primaries and that he is now our President. Aren't you? We must help our President stay out of the Congressional swamp.

Anti-leftist John Doe types have a good message for the country but now their party, the Republicans have chosen not to carry that message on their regular channel. This new "Democrat-Lite" Republican Party idea should fill real Republicans with enough disgust to stop the RINOS.

Yet, in thirty years as I look back, it has not done the trick. My fear, as an anti-leftist, pro-Trump Democrat is that it is not disgusting at all to the leaders of the Republican Party. If I am correct, we are all in more trouble than even most of us think. The big donors have the money that got our representatives elected. Worse than that, the lobbyists, who all are members of the special interests battalion operating out of K-street in Washington DC expect our Representatives to pull all their tricks or they may withhold a great paying job for them when they graduate from Congress. What a swamp!

Unfortunately for good anti-leftist "conservative" Americans, and those non-conservatives who may not realize they benefit from good jobs and fiscal stability, the new Republican attitude does not need you and I to make it work for them. Democrats have convinced this week brood of Republicans that they should see you and I as an embarrassment to the Republican Party. The donors and K-street lobbyists reinforce the disdain of the Republican elite.

I counter that when they express their liberal views about which we disagree whole-heartedly, we are now embarrassed that we ever had faith in such an organization. I know that I no longer have an affinity to the Republican Party.

It is now in the open as bloggers and Talk-Show hosts are hammering Republicans for abandoning once loyal conservatives. The traitors of the R Party still talk about replacing Trump or even undermining him even though he won the Party's nomination and he is now our president. Let us cast the elitists from the Party and rename it with a more American friendly name such as The John Doe Party. Let the others drown in the swamp.

The GOP knows that we, unwashed patriotic Americana, living in front of the locked gates of the extremely prosperous, do not agree with them. Since they continue to lean towards the same progressive agenda as our most un-trusted liberal friends, logic suggests they want us out of their party. I think it is time to go. Just say the word! Let's let President Trump and his whole family lead us to a better place.

All anti-leftists, whether Libertarian, Constitutional, Green, Republican, or even folks like me, bona fide anti-leftist Democrats, should not have to depend on lousy, wimpy, weak, gutless, wussy Republicans to carry our message and fight our fights in the Congress. As we engage with other like-minded American John Does, we must replace the Republican Party with another party which for now, it seems quite proper to label *The John Doe Party*.

After all, Republicans and Democrats have colluded in the name of partisanship to unite to become one blob of nothingness that at its root basics does not care about regular Americans of any ideology. Neither party cares any longer about the American public. Regular Americans are not even small entries on the two-party agenda.

Instead, the corrupt politicians behind these parties choose to trick all Americans into thinking they (the politicians) are the blessing we have sought. It is not true! They advocate principles that would or should make us all want to throw-up. Instead of throwing up, let's do what our parents would have done. Let's throw the bums out! Let them all throw up in their exodus for having been defeated by anti-leftist, pro-American voices. Let President Trump continue to lead us to the promised land as the nominee and President of The John Doe Party.

When you look at the evolution of thought, it is easy to see why Democrats, such as my father, and later myself from the 1960's and 1970's were first conservatives and now we are anti-leftist "conservatives." Anti-leftist is our major ideology and there is a lot of good in conservatism to embrace.

Most of US, who began as Independents or Democrats, have not yet made the switch to Republican because the Republican Party has not been a receptive host for real Americans, who are anti-leftists – not socialists or communists, who still love America.

One thing we must all agree upon however is the fact that those Americans content enough with their lives to take from the US treasury are 99% Democrat and 1% other. Who among them needs real help?

Regular Americans have always wanted to make it on their own. No wonder the US is in such a sad state with the palms of so many American hands facing up, looking for alms, though they have no reason to be poor in the first place. America is not about a handout. It is about a helping hand. More than that, America is about a calloused hand that does the work needed for every day to be a successful work day.

Unfortunately, the Republican Party no longer knows how to connect with most Americans as when it speaks, it speaks mostly to rich donors and lobbyists. Though its core public message is mostly sound, nobody is duped by party leaders who suck up to these factions rather than helping regular John Does in America.

Most people are America-lovers but are lured into periods of progressivism when life does not seem to deal a fair hand.

The bad news for America suggests that Republicans seem to be prepared to lose the next set of elections in Congress, post Trump's election, rather than admit that their base is pro-American and that Donald Trump is a good guy! Being in the anti-leftist "conservative" camp is the only hope for America as it will bring back our economy and give those starving for meaning, a meaningful and high paying job.

Just look at what is happening in the Dakotas if you need proof of how well Americans can do financially in 2017 and in the future.

## Does the R Party want regular John Doe's?

The way I see it, if the Republican Party wanted to represent us, the Party would look at how it really is. Republican leaders would stop plotting against their base and their own candidates. When people really hurt, they need temporary help. They have never needed a lifetime of Obama-like help with a guy like an anti-American Obama in charge of their every move.

The Democrats were outvoted because the next Democrat offered nothing but permanent help, hoping to keep Americans in a state of dependency for political purposes. Americans are not interested in dependency. Americans are and always have been rugged individualists. Our politicians forget this too often.

The Democrat and RINO Republican brand of help condemns a human being to a life of sucking up to government. Republicans will pay dearly in future elections for aligning with Democrats to put forth such an asinine strategy that most real Americans, who work for a living, resent, and are deathly against.

Meanwhile, most Americans are rugged individualists and cannot afford to depend on willy-nilly thought as that which pervades the Republican Party today. For people who are known as stodgy, why the ambivalence? Why not say we love or hate anti-leftist "conservatives," That would help the people to know!

Unfortunately, with no statements, the Republicans lose by default thought. In this case, the default is that RINO Republicans now practice liberal progressivism. And so, another great question is "Who needs a two-party system when both parties offer the same thing?"

Anti-leftist Americans, as all people, have a survival instinct. Republicans, who once espoused conservativism at the grassroots level, are now so ambivalent that even Fox News cannot figure out what Republicans really want to do.

Conservatives have come up with an answer: "Real Republicans apparently do not want conservative Americans in their ranks." Thus, conservatives, *anti-leftists by ideology,* must find an alternative means to save America. Republicans have not been and certainly are not inclined to help. Look only at Mayday, 2017 to get an idea of how far left Republicans have gone.

I have been watching this game for a long time.

Being a small businessman, I have a hard time understanding what motivates the leadership of the Republican Party other than self and selfish interests and gifts from donors and K-street lobbyists.

The Republican Party for years has embraced anti-leftists such as me, though I was a Democrat by registration for most of those years. I have already confessed in this book that when I tried to differentiate conservative from Republican years ago, I defined a real Republican as somebody with over $50 million in the bank. Maybe it was more. Maybe it still is more. Most registered Republican Americans cannot afford to be real Republicans but regular American conservative Republicans had never been treated so small before this brand of RINO leadership got control.

So, my thesis is that Americans without the requisite $50 million in the bank should leave the Republican Party and, along with those of US who are not comfortable in spelling "million"—we should form and join "The John Doe Party."

I see this as the bullet that would soon deprecate the Republican Party as few members of the party have $50 million in the bank, but most are conservatives or at least anti-leftists. How can any political party exist without members? If Republicans want conservatives and normal John Doe Americans in the GOP ever in the future, they would have to reverse their trend towards liberal progressivism. With the recent Omnibus budget on Mayday 2017, I do not see that ever coming. It is probably too late anyway.

Some suggest that the way to win is to out-fund the opposition. Would this not be nice? But if the GOP plays the money game all the time, how can this work for regular John Doe Americans? It cannot!

Ironically the GOP forgets in between elections that it needs those "nasty conservatives." It needs the great unwashed masses in the party to vote for them or they would not have enough people to win any election. If the GOP needs help, they don't show it and they pay little attention to the demands of regular John Doe Americans.

Well too late anyway! All by ourselves, we found Donald Trump. He happens to have his own money and he kicked sixteen other respected Republicans off the stage in the Primary—some with well over $100 million in funding and he is now our President. He beat Hillary Clinton's massive warchest. We made him our President.

From my eyes, the negative consequences to America of the Republican Party's death are greatly exaggerated. I would suggest that along with the $50 million each, Republican elitists should be permitted to swallow and choke on the rest of their wealth. It is annoying to regular Americans that the Republican elite establishment might be intentionally harming America for its own benefit, with help from their new friends across the aisle.

It really upsets me that such otherwise fine human beings (new Republicans who switched just to be with Trump), who can do so much for America, are being treated like they are not welcome by the GOP. It is how they treat us. Regular Americans have had enough. Good-by GOP. Hello John Doe Party

Shame on the leaders of the GOP!

# Chapter 8   The Origin of Political Parties

## American system today gives just two choices.

As many know, in countries around the world, there are often more than just a few political parties. Yet, in the United States there are only two parties that for years have been consistently competitive in elections.

Why is this the case? Are there any prospects of a third party emerging that can possibly be as powerful as the Republicans of 1854? How about a new party, The John Doe Party?

Will anti-leftists and conservatives consider the Reform, Green, Constitutional, or Libertarian Parties? Are these parties competitive with the Democrat and Republican Parties? In our lifetimes, have we ever seen third parties being successful in American politics? No, No, and No again, and unless we do something together, such as form and join The John Doe Party, it will stay that way.

The American system is commonly called a "two-party system" because historically, there have been only two major political parties with candidates competing for offices (especially in federal elections). Many already know that the first two political parties had their origins in the debate over the ratification of the Constitution. In the beginning of the country, there were two factions--the Federalists and the Anti-Federalists.

Today, the Republican and Democratic Parties dominate electoral politics. Almost every federal or state-level elected office in the United States is held by either a Republican or a Democrat. In fact, in the

United States Congress, in 2017, there were only two members in the US Senate who were not either Republican or Democrat.

They are Senator Bernie Sanders of Vermont (The Bern) and Senator Angus King of Maine. Both are independent but they support most of the leftist political whims of the Democrats.

Every other House member and Senator belong to either the Democratic or Republican Party. That gives US an idea of how difficult it would be to run for office without one of the two party's backing. It is still virtually impossible. That is why we need a new party—The John Doe Party.

The deck is stacked against true Americans who simply want to represent their neighbors and friends (constituents) to help the folks back home as well as the country as a whole. Both major parties would gang up on any effort to create a viable, enduring third party, and sometimes they even attack an independent candidate if the candidate has promise.

They may even do things that are illegal if they think they can get away with them or push the notions through the courts system. So, for anti-leftists and conservatives, it will be difficult to break away from the Republican Party but it sure appears that it would be well worth the effort. Things have become intolerable.

Our two-party system is the direct result of the way elections are structured in the United States. Representatives in the Congress and in state legislatures are elected to single-member districts where the individual with the most votes wins. Because only one party's candidate can win in each district, there is a strong incentive for political competitors to organize themselves into two competing "teams" or parties. It saves on money and it saves on effort.

By doing so, party members and their candidates maximize their chances of winning elections. In some counties where there are multi-member districts, parties that win smaller percentages of the vote can often win some legislative representation. Consequently, in such systems, there is an incentive to form smaller "third" parties.

Other features of our system of elections at the highest levels include specific campaign finance rules, an electoral college rather than a direct vote for President, as well as rules giving various candidates ballot access—even write in capabilities. Not much of the laws governing ballot access are fair to regular Americans. They do work fine, however, for entrenched politicians. To learn more about the Electoral College, see amazon.com/author/brianwkelly. Look for a book titled: *The Electoral College for Dummies.*

All of these contrivances are designed by politicians to solidify the two-party system and to provide a distinct advantage for the incumbents from either or both parties. Individuals choosing to buck the system are permitted by the system to join in, but it is designed to make them all fail. Those candidates not sponsored by the elitists in one of the parties are made to look like fools if they choose to confront the constabulary—those who own the election process. The founders never thought Americans would be so slippery and so petty, but alas, we are.

We have all heard the term bi-partisan, which is a duping phrase for voters meaning that when Democrats and Republicans get together to fix things, it is OK. It means that the members of the two supposed hostile parties agree.

Members of two parties violently opposed to each other's notions have chosen to agree on certain matters that are important to citizens. Can you believe that they can do that if the fix is not in? When the parties apparently agree, and the "fix is in," it often means that somebody has been paid off. But, Americans, so wanting our elected representatives to be honest give them the benefit of the doubt.

Americans are too nice. We are inclined to give second chances and so history shows that we have a big problem throwing the bums out of office. Make no bones about it—all of this is our fault and the system will remain corrupt until we say, "Enough!" Then we must follow through with action that changes things.

Americans showed their mettle in electing Donald Trump as President. Now, we must throw back the bums to die in a drained swamp and we must join together to never permit government to get away from us again. We must form The John Doe Party and we must all become active to save our country.

I have experience in messing with the electoral system. I tried to get elected once to each chamber of Congress. I know from this experience that it is an unfair process and that is why we get the candidates we get and that is why wimps get elected to important offices. It is almost impossible for a regular American to get elected to national office unless they are either rich, or they take somebody else's money—I mean a lot of money.

This tacit collaboration of the parties would be called collusion and it would be a crime if two businesses chose to operate that way. Can you imagine Walmart and Sears deciding to use bipartisan logic to fix the prices of similar products, which they sell?

With two parties, the one big advantage is that there can be two distinct points of view, but today with RINO Republicans opting for the Democratic Way, the two-party system is hurting America.  I took no money and I got 17% of the vote in the primary for Congress in PA in 2010, while my competitors each had over $250,000 in their campaign treasuries.

Unfortunately, when our representatives spend so much time together in Washington, it is easy for them to join in unholy alliances of bipartisanship against the American people. These times in America are such times. The damage they do is worse than if Sears and Walmart got together to set prices. Yet there is no law that prohibits both political parties from thinking the same way.

If Sears and Walmart thought the same way, they would be arrested. Collusion or bipartisanship should be looked upon negatively by the people. But, first of course, the people have to begin to realize we are being snookered by corrupt politicians, and we have to be willing to push back against this corruption, or we will see America collapse in front of our eyes.  Donald Trump's rise to prominence is a direct reflection of Americans disgust—being mad as hell—about the collusion of representatives for their own selfish interests.

Having run both for Congress and for the US Senate, I can give testimony that the deck is stacked against anybody without the support of one of the major parties. In other words, those features of our US election system that brought forth the two-party system also serve to effectively block the emergence of third parties or solo efforts by citizens, such as you or me, to seek office.

If you love America as I do, try running for office yourself some time before you get old, if you doubt me. Good candidates without political experience are tacitly excluded from the process. Ironically, most people before the Trump days would see a non-politico such as I running, and they would explain them away as not having experience. If you think about it, experience is an enabler of corruption and so Americans should look for fresh blood, not political hacks to help us solve the corruption problem in Congress and even in lesser offices.

Of course, there are established third parties such as the Libertarian Party, the Green Party, the Constitution Party, and others. Unfortunately, these parties have had little impact on the political process because their concerns have been fragmented among multiple constituencies.

There have been a number of other political parties that have come and gone over the years. History shows that when third parties emerge and hope to be recognized, their successes are short-lived. The Republican party was the last Party to come about and become widely successful. After 160 years, however, as we discussed in the seven chapters before this, it has outlived its usefulness.

Americans must change our way of thinking as the majority are convinced that they would be throwing their votes away if they choose to vote third party v. one or the other two major parties. They may be right. That is why we need The John Doe Party and it is up to all anti-leftist sin the country to make it a huge party.

The lack of success of third parties is true and strong parties such as the Republicans 160 years ago have not emerged because their efforts were not well orchestrated. It is a self-fulfilling prophecy, which we regular people must work to destroy or only crafty politicians will be running for office.

Democrats and Republicans own the landscape and without force of some kind, they are not about to tell the American people that it is a good idea to vote third party. With no unique issues to stand on and then with eventual depleted voter support, third parties generally fade away. But, they do not have to do so, if the people can become energized.

The largest third party since the 1980s is the Libertarian Party, yet even this reasonably popular ideology with a party to match has not had much success in national elections. In the last eighty years, the left and right sides of the political spectrum have been served by the Democrats on the left and the Republicans on the right. Ironically the US political parties are not shaped as the corresponding parties in other parts of the world.

For example, economic liberalism and classical liberalism have a central principle of limited government. Not so in the USA! These notions are supported by anti-leftist conservatives, who traditionally have been allied to the Republican Party in the US, and not to the left-leaning Democratic Party. In other words, liberalism is not liberalism.

As an anti-leftist mostly conservative Democrat, I have never had a deep love for the Republican Party. Yet, being an anti-leftist nationalist and conservative, I have always respected the Republican platform as an alternative to the liberal progressive agenda of the Democrats.

Republicans offered the only anti-leftist game in town that could win a national election. Consequently, rather than vote for progressive liberals, or choose to dilute my vote by going Libertarian, I found myself often voting Republican. A notable exception to this was when I twice supported Robert P. Casey Sr., a respected Pennsylvanian for Governor of Pennsylvania.

I would not support his son, current Senator Robert P. Casey Jr. from PA if dog catcher ever became a political office in our state. I ran against Senator Casey as a write-in Democrat in the PA Senatorial

Primary in 2012. Like most Republicans, Robert P. Casey Jr., a Democrat, is known as a "wimp" in his home town of Scranton PA. This particular apple fell far from the family tree, but Democrats do not care. Casey loves Obama and so he got elected twice. He's up again this year and I sure hope he falls hard. I'll do my best to make sure it happens-- http://www.kellyforussenate.com/. No, I am not running but I left my 2012 site up.

Things have changed in 2017. Like chameleons, many former conservative Republicans, such as RINOs John McCain, and Lindsey Graham, now openly embrace the principles of socialism and liberalism as espoused by the Democratic Party. In America, we are free to be who we wish. My advice on this issue is just don't ever trust them again.

Such faux conservatives, most often called RINOS by real anti-leftist conservatives, have taken control of the Republican Party. Conservatism in general is something Republicans are prepared to abandon. They think they have a better shot at the Hispanic vote without anti-leftists on their team.

Therefore, more and more anti-leftist conservatives are looking for an effective alternative, rather than wasting votes on RINOS. Many are considering the formerly unthinkable. Should we look for a new Party to join? When that decision is made, look for *The John Doe Party.*

I hope to join a new Party, hopefully the John Doe Party, built with American ideals. The new Party should be anti-leftist and nationalist in nature and a perfect name as noted previously would be The John Doe Party. What American would not want to be a member of a great party espousing a pro-American agenda, knowing that it was for America and Americans?

## George Washington was not a two-party politician

Students of history know that George Washington became the first President under the Constitution in 1789, after the Constitution was ratified. There had been other presidents before Washington but not for the new Republic of America with its new Constitution. There were eight Presidents in the thirteen years after America declared its independence and Washington's first term. The list includes patriots John Hancock and John Jay.

Washington served two four-year terms while being a member of no political party. There were no real political parties in Washington's time but that did not mean that all people were in accord on matters that were political in nature.

For example, in Washington's time, there were some issues with John Adams, his Vice President and the second President of the United States. Adams had many disagreements with Thomas Jefferson, Washington's Secretary of State. Adams was a federalist (state's rights) as was Jefferson but they disagreed on many other substantive issues. At the time Alexander Hamilton, a deep American patriot and the author of many of the Federalist Papers, was Secretary of the Treasury.

Additionally, according to the Constitution, candidates for President and Vice President did not run by party affiliation but instead they ran individually. Whichever candidate received the most votes became president and whichever got the second most was elected vice president. When John Adams ran for president upon the expiration of Washington's second term, his identified favored man for the VP job was Thomas Pinckney, but he came in third.  In the third election for President of the US—the election of 1796, Thomas Jefferson, not Pinckney, came in second by only three votes to Adams.

And, so, even without a political party to assure accord at the top of the government, they served together for four years. This was the only time in America's history that political opponents served in the top two executive chairs. It did not mean they had to like each other or always agree.

The election of 1796 was the last time that such a contested American presidential election would occur but this time the President and Vice President were elected from opposing tickets. The two-party system was brewing but the laws gave it no standing. Adams' man did not automatically become Vice President. Instead and it bears repeating, Thomas Jefferson, from the opposing party was the VP in Adams first term. When the Twelfth Amendment to the US Constitution was ratified, such a result became highly unlikely in the future.

As a review, federalism is a political concept in which a group of members are bound together by covenant with a governing representative head. The term "federalism" is also used to describe a system of government such as that used in the United States in which sovereignty is constitutionally divided between a central governing authority (the federal government) and constituent political units (such as states or provinces).

Those who felt as Jefferson believed that states possessed all the rights other than those rights which they freely might choose to give to the federal government, were known as the Jeffersonians.  For comic relief, please note they were not known as the "Jefferson's."

They also believed in the full authority of the body of laws known as the Constitution. Just as anti-leftist conservatives today, the followers of Jefferson believed that a powerful central government posed a big threat to individual liberties. Their view was that the US was a confederation of sovereign entities (the states) which chose to band together for their common good, without giving the central group power over the parts. In essence, the common thought was that the states "owned" the Federal Government, and not vice versa.

Alexander Hamilton, another great patriot, who is known to have written many of the Federalist Papers leading up to the ratification of the Constitution, had a contrary opinion. He argued that a strong central government was a very good thing and in fact it was essential to the unity of the new nation. The Hamilton contingent favored a broad interpretation of the Constitution. They saw the document as something that should and would evolve with the country as it grew.

I took time several years ago to break up the huge multi-page sentences of the Federalist Papers and I produced a book published by Lets Go Publish! titled: *The Federalist Papers by Hamilton, Jay, & Madison*. I also wrote a small companion book to put the papers in perspective. It is titled *The Federalist Papers Companion*.  Of course, I would recommend both. They sell well on Amazon and Kindle.

Political parties were not something that the founders as well as other leading political figures of the new country, including George Washington, were concerned about. They were happy without them. They believed that having political parties, such as the Whigs, and the Tories as they existed in England, would polarize citizens and paralyze government.

Look at the Democrats and the Republicans today to see why they had such great concerns. When the parties as today, go along to get along, the American people are the ones who feel the pain of their compromises.

Look what has happened to the Republicans and Democrats today. Hamilton and Jefferson both agreed with this notion. However, by the mid 1790's the two groups that they represented became separated by other ideologies and they had broken apart into separate factions. Hamilton's group became known as the "Federalists," while Jefferson's faction became the "Democratic Republicans." It is easier to refer to them as the "Jeffersonians."

The Jeffersonians differed strongly with the Hamiltonians on economic matters. The Democratic-Republicans believed in protecting the interests of the little guys -- working classes such as merchants, farmers, and laborers. They felt that an agrarian economy would best serve the regular citizens as opposed to the elites. There were no iPads or Smart Phones back then.

They did not like the idea of the establishment of a national bank of the United States (Hamilton strongly favored its establishment). They felt that such a mechanism, as our Federal Reserve Bank could be a means of usurping power that belonged to individual states. They were also concerned that such a bank would be tied too closely to the rich, and then again, the national government. They feared that people in a central government would become too powerful.

Of course, Jefferson was right, but a compromise with Hamilton would have perhaps kept the ideologues from clashing over the subsequent years.

The Federalists saw industry and manufacturing as the best means of domestic growth and economic self-sufficiency. They favored the existence of protective tariffs on imports (Congress adopted these in 1789), both as a means of protecting domestic production and as a source of revenue. This is still a good idea and recently I wrote two books, RRR, and Saving America, both of which recommend a return to these forms of mercantilism that originally made our country strong.

## Our two-party system does not have to be!

It is probably obvious in this chapter that the two-party system is not required by the Constitution. As noted above, a number of patriots were in fact openly hostile to the idea of political parties. George Washington was one of them and he of course is quoted as being worried about the "baneful effects of the spirit of party" on the young Republic. Jefferson was even blunter in his criticism: "If I could not go to heaven but with a party, I would not go there at all."

Originally as discussed in this chapter, Hamilton and Adams won out over Jefferson but Jefferson would have his day. Ironically, Hamilton had a hard time getting his ideas across and adopted without having like-minded men on his side.  So, to win passage of his programs, he formed coalitions with men of like minds and together these allies as noted became known as the Federalists. They recruited candidates to be successful in subsequent elections so as to increase their majority in the Congress.

Not to be outdone by others who did not want a reenactment of the English style Whigs and Tories on the American landscape, Madison and Jefferson, who were opponents of Hamilton's policies, formed their own political party as noted in this chapter.

The Federalists as they existed back then, were in many ways like the Democrat Party of today in that they believed in a strong central government, whereas the new Jeffersonian Democratic-Republicans believed that the federal government lacked the constitutional authority to implement Hamilton's agenda.

In many ways, they were like the strong-hearted Republicans of about ten or twenty or thirty years ago. They were very much like the anti-leftist conservatives of today. Because the Republicans are no longer who they once were, as I suspect you already know, I have been compelled to write this book. Would I not enjoy counsel from the great ones – Jefferson, Washington, Hamilton, and Madison? Can you imagine their perspective?

Ironically, the Democrats, as they would eventually become known, supported an agrarian-based economy that promoted the well-being of farmers and tradesmen. They were originally for successful industry but not for large businesses dominating the culture or large government taking what it wanted in taxes.

They sure do not sound like today's liberal progressive Democrats and this explains why our parents (I am a Democrat) had no problem being Democrats. At one time, they were the true party of the people. Today, Democrats are the party of the socialist / progressives and the communists, and any citizen operating in a fringe area. Democrats no longer try to get the white vote. When I understood that was true, I questioned why, being white, would I be a loyal Democrat.

Democrats today love constituents who are happy with destroying America with a huge Robin-Hood type government in which the objective is to make the people dependent on the government. I am waiting for the John Doe Party before I leave the Democrat Party. However, it would be nice if in the meantime, I could help Democratic leadership move to a different line of thinking. Yet, I am not holding my breath on Democrats ever changing.

The Democratic-Republicans were successful shortly after they were formed. In the election of 1800, they scored their first victory. Jefferson defeated John Adams in Adams' second attempt at the highest office in the land.

Encouraged by its success, the Democratic-Republican Party began organizing at the state and local level as well. Within just a few years, the D-R Party had become the dominant political party in the US. The egghead, Brainiac Federalists did not connect with the electorate and they appeared to represent only the elite and the wealthy portions of the American people, though this was not a fully accurate description.

Clearly there were far more people than successful people and so what Democratic Republicans could not achieve economically, they were able to achieve at the ballot box. In 1816, the Federalists were finished as they fielded their last presidential candidate, who lost in a landslide to James Monroe.

During his terms, President Madison (1809 to 1816), a Democratic Republican had succeeded in realizing certain big measures favored by the Federalists, for example a national bank and protective tariffs. This gave the Federalists in 1816 few issues to campaign on. This resulted in the overwhelming victory of James Monroe for the Democratic-Republicans in a battle against the Federalist nominee Rufus King of New York. This was just about the end of the Federalists.

## Tid bits of the two-party system on the way to today

In a two-party system, just like in a basketball game, certain parties go on a run and win election after election, while the opposition party keeps losing. For example, let's jump ahead to the time between 1932 and 1980. The Democrats won seven of 11 presidential contests, and held both chambers of Congress for all but a few years. Yes, that means that the Republicans lost 4 of 11.

Backing up, as noted, the fledgling US got to test its constitutional precepts on elections way back in the elections of the late 1700's. The third one was really historic. It was one of the first peaceful transfers of power between opposing political parties ever in the political history of the world. It was certainly a first in a democracy (democratic republic).

The victorious Democratic-Republican Party were perhaps as surprised as anybody that power transferred without a fight. As an aside, as we have been promulgating so far in this book, the Democratic-Republican Party was a direct predecessor of the modern Democratic Party, and thus it is considered to be the oldest continuous political party in the world.

Soon after the 1824 election, the Democratic-Republican Party officially split into the National Republicans (led by Adams and Henry Clay) and the Democratic Party (led by Jackson).

The notion of national conventions was not far off once the US political parties started to blossom into their current shape. The conventions were intended to galvanize party members for the coming election. The Democrats held their first-ever national convention in 1832. It was convened in Baltimore, Maryland, more or less as a big pep rally.

However, since there were always factions within parties, its upbeat tempo helped smooth over differences between several Party factions, and the principals and the delegates were able to rally the Party behind a single candidate for president.

The purpose of the convention was to choose a running mate for incumbent President Andrew Jackson. Secretary of State Martin Van Buren was nominated for Vice President and the convention endorsed Jackson's reelection. The first US convention of all time accomplished its mission.

Before the prototype of today's Republican Party came into being, a phenomenon in the 1840s and 1850s, known as the *Know-Nothing Party,* which many called The American Party, competed with the splintered off Republicans to replace the Whig Party to become the Democrats' major opposition.

Sergeant Schultz of Hogan's Heroes was not the founder of the "Know Nothings." As we all know, the infamous Schultz is well known for saying: "I know nothing!"

The Know-Nothings got their name because their membership was sworn to secrecy. They were permitted to say nothing but: I know nothing about it, when asked of their party affiliation. At one point, the Know-Nothings included in their ranks six governors, five senators, and 43 House members.

# Chapter 9  Founding of the GOP & Its Long Success

## Who's who—early politics—Democrats & the Whigs!

With the demise of the Federalists, who ironically at the time were emulating today's Democrats in their desire for a strong central government, while they also favored the rich and the elites, the newly empowered Democratic-Republicans began to dominate the political landscape. With the split during Andrew Jackson's times, the Democrat side of the split began to prosper. Life was so good, or so it seemed at the time, that President Monroe's term of office became known as the "era of good feeling."

Ironically, things were so good that the people stopped paying attention to politics and eligible voter turnout dropped dramatically—from more than 40 percent in 1812 to less than 10 percent in 1820. Voters felt they had little reason to go to the polls since the highly successful Democratic-Republican Party had decimated the Federalists and had brought them what appeared to be Nirvana even before Kurt Cobain.

No group of people can get along forever without a common enemy. With the Federalists out of the way, the Democratic-Republican Party began to squabble among themselves, much like the Republicans of today, who can't figure out left from right. Eventually, factions formed within the Party. They were as devastating to the health of the Party as if the Party had split in two.

To reflect the divisiveness within the Democratic-Republican Party, in the presidential election of 1824 the Party had five candidates ready to succeed James Monroe. War hero Andrew Jackson (War of 1812) won the popular vote. However, due to the Electoral College and the notion of delegates v. the popular vote, Jackson failed to receive a majority of electors.

Thus, to settle the squabble, the election was to be decided by the House of Representatives. In this interesting test of Democracy and the Constitution in action, runner-up John Quincy Adams, the son of the second President, become the victor by forging a deal with third-place finisher Henry Clay.

Jackson's supporters understandably were upset by what they saw as backroom deal-making, and splintered off to form what they called the "Democratic Party." They revived an old Jeffersonian coalition of farmers and tradesmen, and began to effectively organize at the national, state, and local level. They formed clubs and committees, holding rallies, established a chain of newspapers, and they raised a lot of money for their candidates. This technique can be used again as the secret to a successful John Doe Party organization. We can learn lots from the past.

The rallying cry of the new Democratic Party was the elimination of corruption in Washington. Wouldn't that be nice! The more things change the more they stay the same. Think of what the Republicans would be able to do if their backers chose to control the media by purchasing news outlets. But, unfortunately for America, Republicans in 2016 / 2017 have chosen to continue to be the "Wimp Party," and the elites with the money seem content that Democrats dominate the media.

Supporters of President John Quincy Adams, however, did not stand still. They responded by collecting together the rest of the factions of the Democratic-Republican Party and they joined with the outraged remnants of the old Federalist Party. They picked a poor name (Whigs) but their idea is as sound today as would be the John Doe Party when we are ready to pull it off.

Unfortunately, just as today, the Whigs, as they became known, lacked the Democrats' organization skills, and drive. They were soundly defeated in 1828, 1832, and 1836. They scored their only presidential victories in 1840 and 1848 with war heroes William Henry Harrison and Zachary Taylor, respectively.

The wins had little to do with the party message and lots to do with their outstanding candidates. The Whig Party was doomed by its own ineptness—the same kind of ineptness and lack of purpose that is already dooming the Republican Party.

In many ways, the new parties held the same ideologies as their forerunners. Those on opposite camps did not trust each other a bit. However, they were quite consistent in their economic policy.

The new Whigs supported a national bank and tariffs as did the old Federalists. They hoped to protect manufacturers and use industry to keep the country strong.  The Democrats were against the central bank and they were for low tariffs since this helped the farmers sell their wares abroad—even though they caused non-agrarian US employees to work for companies that were hurt by lower priced imported products.

Both parties were badly split over the slavery issue. Consequently, since they did not want it to be a debate point, the parties colluded to suppress slavery from becoming a national issue, as many in the R and D parties do today regarding abortion. Despite not wanting to talk about slavery, just as abortion today, it proved impossible as feelings and emotions intensified.

## The Modern Democrats and the Modern Republicans

Through this book, I continue to encourage anti-leftist nationalists to form and then join the John Doe Party as the natural way to diminish and eventually eliminate the Republican Party for ostracizing anti-leftists and conservatives. Why? History is repeating itself as today's RINOS are led by a group of elitists much like the Whigs. Thus, the solution can be the same and it should happen today exactly as it happened in 1854.  Yes, it can happen again in 2018 and in 2020. There was no Republican Party until the Whigs bit the dust, and there is yet to be a John Doe Party with strength enough to win until we all help the Republicans bite the dust.

Where there is opposition, there is opportunity. The Whigs were not much more than the old Federalist Party and their reluctance to discuss slavery became a big issue. In many ways, it was their undoing.

In 1854, a group of anti-slavery forces organized to form a third party. Out of the political party archives, they dug up the other half of the old name "Democratic-Republicans," and they took the other half as their moniker. They became the "Republicans."

There was no trace of a biased or corrupt media back then as there is today. Consequently, the regular people were not induced to hate Republicans simply because they were Republicans. Instead, the Republicans quickly attracted anti-slavery members from both of the two major parties. They also absorbed the pro-business elements of the dying Whig coalition. This is the same approach that can make The John Doe Party an overnight success.

## The first Republican candidate for president

The first presidential candidate of the new Republicans was a man named John Fremont. He is not well known in history, and was not exceedingly popular in his day. Fremont was soundly defeated in the elections of 1856.

After regrouping from this initial loss, the Republican Party put forth its second candidate for President, a humble man named Abraham Lincoln. Lincoln was victorious in the election of 1860 and the world changed forever. It will change again when conservatives in both the Democratic and the Republican parties of today, along with conservative Libertarians, Constitutionals, Greens, Reforms, and other parties choose to join together to form The John Doe Party. Donald Trump would make a great first President from The John Doe Party in 2020, don't you think?

The success of the Republican Party with Abraham Lincoln was monumental. Most minorities, blacks and even Hispanics, think the Democrats ended slavery, but it was the Republicans. Abraham Lincoln was their man. Lincoln was not a Democrat. The Republican Party became the first and only third party in American history to ascend to major party status. I am counting on The John Doe Party to be the next!

Today, the lying progressives and liberals in the Democrat Party have used propaganda to convince the American youth and the voters who do not pay attention that the very name "Republican Party" is reason enough to vote Democrat. This theme is a theme representing the extent of the corruption of the media.

The young in America today, often called the millennials, have voted in an idealist movement that is bent on destroying all opportunity for young Americans. It is ironic that the millennials have voted for diminished personal opportunities, while receiving nothing at all in return. Coffee breathed university professors have espoused Dumb and Dumber as the models for the millennials and "babes in the woods" have fallen for the message of the progressives. "Government is the only God."

Thus, millennials have no compelling need to vote for candidates who favor young Americans like themselves. Instead, they imbecilically follow the instructions of their coffee breath professors to avoid favoring a party that is working for them to graduate with high paying jobs—one that wants America and all Americans, especially the young to succeed. And, so millennials are very unsuccessful as a group and most live with their parents after graduating from college. They literally are reaping the bad crop from the seed they elected.

And so, along with many low information Americans, the "independently minded" millennials vote Democrat consistently and mindlessly, because their coffee-breath professors tell them to do so. This of course places them and their to-be progeny on the road to big time failure.

Meanwhile, their liberal progressive parents, with whom they are forced to live since they cannot find meaningful work or any work at all, cannot understand the cause and effect nature of life. So much can change at the ballot box but the idealists refuse to see it, and they continue to vote with their hearts instead of their heads, and their children continue to suffer.

It would be nice if the Democrats had a plan to make the economy of the US vibrant again. Even without a plan it would be nice if they joined the opposition to work for America.

They prefer that millennials and others continue to have deep gratitude to big government for giving them food stamps and cell phones and other goodies, rather than giving them positive prospects for a good life, and a real opportunity to achieve it. Donald Trump is already changing the scenario for the better, but it will take time for millennials to be deprogrammed from the raunchy smell of coffee-breath.

Ironically, the youth borrow money from the government and go to school. Then when they graduate, they cannot find a job, partly because while in school they voted against the pro-jobs candidates.

For years, their far-left coffee-breath professors continued to blame George Bush because it was convenient yet no employer cared about how much the graduates hated the former President. Now, they blame Donald Trump while it is the same professors who are the perpetrators of this sorry trick upon young American hopefuls.

The same employers care nothing about how much the new graduates hate the new President. And, so they quickly become members of the unemployed. It is a simple cause and effect matter. Coffee-breath professors teach them it is OK to take government handouts, rather than become self-sufficient and so many millennials do not learn the skills needed to get and hold jobs.

Where are Republicans on this travesty? Why have the Republicans not explained the cause and effect to theoretically bright college graduates, rather than just sit down and take it?  Republicans are MIA on just about everything that can help defeat Democrats and on what is right for the USA.  They were too busy protecting themselves from a Donald Trump presidency because his plans would make America fair again and the elite establishment would no longer be the party bosses. Now, they are busy delegitimatizing the President as he tries to drain the swamp of them and their cohorts.

## What happened to Republicans after Lincoln?

We all seem to know the history of the two major political parties after the Civil War. From the time of the War, Republicans dominated national politics from 1860 to 1932, controlling Congress for most of that time. They won all but four presidential elections. During this period, the Republicans stood for making America strong.

They espoused policies good for America. They brought forth national expansion, and laissez-faire (free market) capitalism. Without the sanity that the Republicans brought to the American business climate, Americans today would be speaking German, Russian, or Chinese, and perhaps all three just to buy a bar of soap.

The Democrats were the party of immigrants, farmers, and tradesmen, or so it seemed. Yet, many Democrats worked in the factories, including the auto workers, and they made as much money as many white collared Republicans. How soon we forget what good industry brings to a country.

Today, Republicans have forgotten their own message, and that is why nobody knows how good they can be. Today, Republican wimps in the leadership roles in the Party do not permit anti-leftist conservatives or the rest of their membership to climb out from under their school-desks.

Since Republicans cannot hear or will not hear the voices of the anti-leftists and anti-elites, and anti- swampers, pushing them to man-up, it is surely the right time to bring on The John Doe Party. Most of the Republican base and a substantial portion of the Democratic base are poised to become The John Doe Party. Let's make it happen together.

# Chapter 10  Twentieth Century Presidents

## The Wilson years

On the way to FDR, there was nobody besides Woodrow Wilson who did more for socialism and progressivism than any other president. Wilson fully enabled a revenue source that kept on giving for the Wilsonian notion of redistribution of wealth. Wilson never asked, "Where's the beef?" He knew that it existed in the Personal and Corporate Income Taxes that he made happen while he was president. Wilson was the guy that got to distribute it all.

Just like I was forced to suffer from January 2009 to January 2017, I cannot think of something more desired by conservatives and anti-leftists in his time than Woodrow Wilson's term having expired. Americans had to put up with Wilson from March 4, 1913 – March 4, 1921. I suspect a few good Americans, not necessarily the elites, dropped full kegs of tapped American beer on the streets when Wilson's financial reign of terror on the working class ended. Ten they tapped them, celebrated and drank the beer. Why lie?

The Personal Income Tax brought in under the Wilson regime was the source of funding that took the earnings of hard working Americans and gave them to those who had not earned the wages. This was once known as "relief" but now is known as redistribution of income just as Obamacare became known as redistribution of healthcare from those who had healthcare to those who had never earned it.

Americans have always been chumps for sob stories and Wilson and Obama and the Democrats were full of them and other things that hurt the sustenance of the country.

Wilson's adoption of the Personal Income Tax gave all presidents from that point on in history, the opportunity to use the public's money for social engineering endeavors. All such schemes are against the Constitution but this did not matter to Wilson, FDR, LBJ, or the last bad President, Barack H. Obama. With lots of revenue from the new income tax levy, Wilson was able to achieve his goal of using "practical means of realizing for society the principles of socialism" by unshackling state power.

Before he exited, Obama was never as bold as Wilson to announce his principles but they were the same nonetheless. If you did not want to depend on the Government for your entire life, neither Wilson nor Obama in their time had little to offer. President Trump actually offers a great life for all who wish to engage in life's great activities, including work.

Wilson had a radical political agenda but was unable to achieve all of his socialist objectives in two terms--but he tried. He caused a lot of lasting damage nonetheless. His revitalized democratic political science notions addressed the issues he identified. Wilson had a "different" view of policy, organization, and administration and he brought this view to his actions through his long career in the academy and in politics, and as president.

Having eradicated the significance of individual rights for democracy in his writings, Wilson went on to decree that the Constitution was not the final word. He was not a fan of the Constitution and he strongly advocated eliminating the separation of powers. From his perspective, just like Roosevelt and Obama ruling by Executive Orders, Wilson hoped he could unleash unlimited majority party government for his Party. Wilson, though a Democrat believed he could bring practicality to the demands of socialism, and he openly suggested that socialism should be the ruling ideology of his Party—the Democrat Party.

Thankfully, America is structured to survive people like Woodrow Wilson, Lyndon Baines Johnson, Franklin D. Roosevelt, and Barack H. Obama, and their innate desire to crush America, the land of the free.

Wilson would have done well as President of the USSR. Over time, poor leaders such as Wilson and Barack Hussein Obama are apt to appear, hoping to take all Americans down a trail that the founders never imagined. We avoided another tyrant by saying no to Hillary Clinton and saying yes to an American President who loves America, Donald J. Trump.

# The Roosevelt years

One can make a great argument that the two-party system has not served America so well, yet even those founders that wanted no parties recognized that a "no party" system simply could not work for politicians. The current system therefore is rigged for politicians by politicians and ballot access is denied regular citizens by elite lawmakers from both of the main parties.

If great minds from many political parties were permitted into the power structure during the Great Depression, and if their ideas were truly evaluated, Roosevelt could not have postponed the US post-depression recovery as he did, until his death.

Few of US can name even a few things that politicians do well, other than breathe, consume resources, and spend other people's money. Try running for any elected office, and you will quickly see that the political classes, who inherently are incapable of governing, are very capable of creating a thousand obstacles for any regular American to be elected to serve the public.

Look at the trouble Donald Trump had getting elected with the traditional elitists from his own party. He surely is a breath of fresh air for America. Americans hope that this new President gives nothing to the swamp. Remember, Mr. Trump, your pledge was to drain it, not swim in it!

Some call Franklin Roosevelt's victory in 1932 as a "realignment" of the political parties. The Great Depression was in full bloom, and Herbert Hoover had had a tough time making things better for Americans. Liberals would say that the Republican policies of industrialization, high tariffs, and unregulated commerce caused the depression, and when they were replaced by Roosevelt's New Deal, things got better. This unfortunately was not the case for many poor Americans, but just like when Obama and the sycophant press ran the daily news, Roosevelt did not let bad news leak out of his White House.

The New Deal was characterized by many as a patchwork of federal spending programs and government regulations designed to create a social safety net for low-income Americans, particularly union workers, who loved making the Roosevelt political coffers swell.

Though there were breadcrumbs for new immigrants, minorities, and small-business owners, there was little cause and effect improvement. Eventually everything got better when the war economy began. Even Roosevelt could not prevent true economic prosperity.

However, Roosevelt is not credited with all the major solutions during his 12 + years. He sure was the war President from 1939 to 1943 and then he was elected for his fourth term while the war was still in full bloom in 1944. He was clearly America's commander in chief and a great hero during WWII.

Few Americans did not credit Roosevelt for America and the allies winning the big war. Just six months ago, before Donald Trump became our president, Barack Obama seemed quite pleased to be able to play footsie with our enemies. Hillary Clinton as Secretary of State did the same and because Americans knew she would do more damage if elected president, Americans who love America cut her off at the pass.

By the end of WWII, the USA had placed the Great Depression in the annals of past history and from its war manufacturing prowess, the country became one of the most powerful nations in the world. Nobody could compete with America. Of course, Harry Truman a great Democrat who loved America more than his party, was President at the war's end. FDR passed away on April 12, 1945, about five months before Truman ended the war.

# Sometime great decisions need to be made by great people.

The Commander in Chief for most of WWII, FDR, was almost perfect in the war as he used all of his domestic talents, including fireside chats to lead the war effort. He was inspirational. The people were convinced he was the right guy at the right time. He enlisted the support of the American people on the Radio to help win the war. He was a great cheerleader but with sincerity.

If he had another motive in his Fireside speeches other than what was best for America, it was undetectable by normal people as well as a press that was quite discerning at the time. He was simply a hero in this regard and most Americans either never blamed him or forgave him for all of his poor economic policies. After the War, the economy boomed, as American industry was ready for a post-war restart. The economy not only restarted, it boomed. America was on top again.

Like many before him, Roosevelt's war record was not perfect. But, there are few historians that suggest that if somebody other than Franklin D. Roosevelt were president, the war would not have gone so well for the US and its allies. Yet, none of these war successes ever made FDR a great economist.

Without the war, there are a number of economists who suggest that Roosevelt, just like our prior president, Barack H. Obama, actually stopped the country from recovering sooner by whacking the producing class and limiting the number of jobs. If that sounds like Mr. Obama's and Ms. Clinton's probable recipe for success, just as in the Roosevelt days, there would be no jobs coming any time soon. But, in our times, the people said "no," and the people decided to trust Donald J. Trump to lead America.

And, if I may, the people are really annoyed at Democrats demeaning their duly elected President and the Republicans getting in the way of the people's agenda. Get out of the way in 2017 and thereafter as Trump is our commander and chief A bunch of anti-Trumpists will not be tolerated by the people of America. Remember The John Doe Party is a lasting answer.

Roosevelt needed the war and he needed Harry Truman to end it so that Americans could get back to work. Obama, when he had the opportunity did not seem to think it was worth anybody's effort to step in to help America, whether Americans were working or not, as long as his own political future was assured,

## What caused the Great Depression? Why did it take so long to recover?

Thinking through why we never got out of the Great Depression until the massive war buildup put everybody back to work, what could have been done differently?  There are a number of theories as to what caused the major depression and what might have been done to help escape from this period of no hope, which is so similar to what we now experience.

Some suggest that there are **Keynesian economic theories** of demand that explain it clearly. Many quietly agree that it was the stock market crash that caused Americans to lose confidence in the ability of the country to recover. Keynesians however profess the same economic ideology that for the last eight years guided Obama into being 100% ineffective. They argued that businesses had over invested anticipating additional business and when it did not come, they were forced to cut back.

There are lots of other notions. Some exonerate Roosevelt as not really understanding the economic forces in play and others would choose to castrate him as they believe he did.

Marxists of course have their own point of view. They suggest that the Great Depression was merely a big symptom of the inherent instability of the capitalist model. One thing we all know with certainty; it took a war to end the great depression and nobody wants a great war to begin the Trump road to recovery.

# Chapter 11   RINOS Ruined the Republican Party

## Is the divorce final?

How much do anti-leftists have in common with the Republicans of today? The fact that the question is put forth begs the response: "Not much!" Anti-leftist conservatives are not about to negotiate limits to our freedom by changing the bill of rights to give government more power, even if it upsets our one-time allies, the Republicans and their friends the RINOS.

Why would any American want to relinquish individual freedom to a tyrannical government wanting to keep Americans under its control? I hope I do not have to answer that!

In his well-publicized interview in summer 2013 with Greta Van Susteren, formerly of Fox News, Rush Limbaugh acknowledged the rift between conservatives and Republicans but he sees it as something even larger. He sees the Republicans and Democrats becoming like-minded almost like there is now just one Party. Here is Rush in his own words:

*"And I don't think it's so much conservative versus liberal, although it is, but it's Washington versus the rest of the country is what's really transpiring now. And Washington has a mindset and a desire for the country that doesn't dovetail with the majority of the American people."*

Though Rush Limbaugh, the true voice of anti-leftist sentiment in America today, did not at one time think that a new party would help matters, he is not totally against it. His original thinking was that it would be better for conservatives to fight for and win the leadership positions in the Republican Party and make it the party for anti-leftist conservatives. So far with Trump as the theoretical leader of the Party, the anti-Trumpists in Congress and the donor class, are plotting to undermine the Trump presidency.

And, so, I say, let the RINOS find another Party. If getting leadership positions could have worked, it would have worked already in the four years that have passed. We now see that even with the Presidency of Donald Trump, there is no reconciliation. Republican elites, their powerful donors and K-street friends have not ceded anything to anti-leftist conservatives, or nationalists and instead they have dug in to undermine the Trump presidency.

Thus, the talk about forming The John Doe Party is long overdue as we anti-leftist nationalists are getting hammered by Republicans at every turn, and there are no doors opening for any of us to have a larger voice in Party decisions. It took a billionaire, Donald Trump to crash through the elite establishment barrier to be in a position to represent the real people in this country instead of the power brokers and political donors. Thank God for that!

The TEA Party had been rendered mostly ineffective by the mainstream media with their reputation-destroying attacks on Sarah Palin along with Karl Rove's and other establishment types' disdain for non-elites. It still exists but is muted as the President cannot get help from Congress to get the American Agenda passed.

The moms and dads and uncles and aunts who once tuned in as silent members of the TEA Party are still very upset and instead of joining anything, they simply voted to effect change. Donald Trump did not just happen. It was grassroots anti-leftist nationalists and populists—those who love America who brought him the nomination and the presidency.

When The John Doe Party is brought forth as an entity and not just a great thought, it will steal 99% of Republicans, many Democrats, and most Independents. Substantial parts of the Libertarians, Greens, and the Constitution Party will also sign up. They will all go willingly. The TEA Party that is left at that time will also climb aboard and quickly be absorbed by The John Doe Party.

In fact, I would suspect that some important John Doe Party leaders will come from the TEA Party. Perhaps a candidate for President from The John Doe Party will show up from the ranks of the TEA Party to help us all create The John Doe Party that we all desire, and one that will succeed! My desire would be to have Donald Trump as the first John Doe Party President four years from now.

The Republican Party has stood for over 160 years from when conservatives abandoned the Whigs and the intrinsic evil of slavery that they promulgated. Republican Abolitionists began their success by getting Abraham Lincoln elected as the President of the USA.

Lincoln ultimately preserved the Union and freed men and women of color from the bondage of slavery. The reasons why this Party wants to purge anti-leftists and those not carrying an elitist badge, is not fully understood and it is not within the Party's founding. It was once a great party in the mid 1900's. The Republican Party has now become an unfortunate reincarnation of the Whig Party with a leaning towards progressivism. It has lost its value to regular Americans who love America.

The facts are clear that a cadre of Faux anti-leftists such as John McCain, Mutt Romney, Jeb Bush, Lyndsey Graham, Karl Rove and other elite RINOS, who hail from the Republican Party, cannot be entrusted to preserve the values of regular Americans. With their anti-Trump rhetoric, joining with the Democrats, they prove it every day. How can John Doe Americans work with people who are not really on our side?

They have sold out basic American principles for the comfort of getting along with the person across the aisle and the Washington lobbyists and donor class and the elite Republicans. They do not value our existence within the Party and are giving US less and less voice. They'd like us to leave and we should take their message and exit quickly.

Will they drink the tonic of Americanism again and become cured? Don't hold your breath! Republicans will go the way of the Whigs when left without those anti-leftists who were once labeled "conservatives."

My prediction is that these elites may eventually become powerful members of the Democratic Party. Good riddance!

A number of years ago I was puzzled that so many regular Americans of small means were members of the Republican Party, the traditional party of big business and industry. It made little sense to me at a dollars and cents level. This was before the open emergence of a left wing of elite establishment types in leadership positions of the Republican Party.

Even now, from the time of the Republican Primary of 2016, I saw regular Americans signing out from the Democratic Party and their raunchy liberalism and signing up with the clean, better living, better ethics, better morals of the Republican Party simply so they could vote for Donald Trump. My sister-in-law and others in my family and circle of friends made the transition and they do not regret it.

They were becoming American nationalists, pro-American regular John and Jane Does and the Republicans at the time were the most convenient party to accept their views on life. Republicans unfortunately are no longer there. That is why The John Doe Party will be very successful.

I ask myself as a Democrat, what is a real Republican – one who has the power to influence the Party? None of my friends working in sweat shops or in menial white collar jobs fit that bill. As I thought it through, I saw Republicans running small businesses and large businesses with great success. Yet, I wondered about the small business owners with just about $1million in assets as to how influential even they could be in the money-rich Republican Party at the National Level.

So, I took a stab at it. I defined a Republican as someone with over $50 million in wealth who wants more, and who has some means to achieve it that depends often on positive government policy. These real Republicans do need the willingness of the little people to both fund their political aspirations and to provide votes, which they would not otherwise get because their true numbers are very small. That's really about it.

So, now, it seems that Republicans think they can do their magic without having the regular John Doe values that attract the small-time voters such as me. The GOP elites would be happy of course if I would simply agree to vote for them no matter what their platform might be, and I would permit them to take a bit of my money for their cause.

I always wondered why that worked and I think it is because most people who want to be good people lean conservative v progressive. Progressives to be true have no God but the state. Yet, most progressives are not told that by their corrupt leaders. Those who switched from D to R are anti-leftists for sure. Don't tell that to a liberal—but it is the truth.

Unfortunately, Republicans are messing up their deal with the little people – the anti-leftist John Does from Realville. The new mantra of the RINO Republicans who control the Party today is to become chummy with the big government left. This will not work because the less important people they leave behind are not low-information voters – just the opposite. They are high information voters, and they will leave the Republican Party as soon as they see that it has sold them out. Where will they go? The John Doe Party, of course.

The old, people-first GOP is gone for good. It is difficult to believe; but it is true. There is no reason for regular Americans to stick around and support a GOP elite leadership that plans to sell us all and our posterity back into thralldom. To the logical American mind, it is far more advantageous for the furthering of the American cause to form a workable third party that will be immediately popular.?

There should be more options on the table than the tyranny-lite that the Republicans are peddling nowadays. The John Doe Party offers hope for a really exciting and productive future for anti-leftists and conservatives and for all Americans of good will.

May God give US our opportunity!

# Chapter 12   The John Doe Party

## Party of Americans for the good of Americans

There has never been a national conservative party per se but politically independent Fox News correspondent Sean Hannity tells us he is a registered member of the Conservative Party of New York. Hannity quit the Republican Party about ten years back because he is a conservative and he was disgusted with the McCain presidential campaign.

He saw gentleman John McCain and other RINO Republicans taking control of the Republican Party and it did not look well for anti-leftist conservatives. Donald Trump changed the notion of conservatism by making it simply Americans for America. America First! Most conservatives always thought that was what it was all about anyway, and so without alienating those who are not died in the wool conservatives, the Trump way is Nationalism with a little splash of conservatism and a whole lot of anti-leftism added in for good measure.

Many conservatives learned during the Trump campaign that we were more pro-American than we were conservative. The word for that is nationalist. We John Does are not elites. We are not establishment, and yes, we have good American values. Donald Trump represented most of our values and yet he was not a full conservative and some might say he was not even a half conservative. Rush Limbaugh recognized this first and every now and then he reminds us such as last week:

"How many times during the campaign did I warn everybody Trump is not a conservative? Multiple times a day. How many times a day did I tell people that Donald Trump is not even ideological? Multiple times a day. How many times have I told you, do not expect Trump to be a conservative; he isn't one. Why did I change the name of my think tank from the Institute for Advanced Conservative Studies to the Institute for Advanced Anti-Leftist Studies?"

One thing all Trump supporters have in common is that we are all anti-leftist, the dogma of the Democrats. For many, being anti-leftist has a lot of room for conservatism. Even Trump on many issues appears to be a conservative but he is merely practicing his America-First philosophy.

The new John Doe Party will take all anti-leftists, and just about all conservatives, nationalists, and populists as well as those from other parties that are also fed up with progressives pushing the limits of sanity. Hillary Clinton clearly represented the status quo and that provided even more impetus for Americans to make Donald Trump our President.

The John Doe Party will become the largest party ever and it will bring a great America back for all of us. It will be the party of America for Americans. For purposes of this chapter, when we say conservative or nationalist or populist or America lover, we mean all types of potential new members of The John Doe Party. America-first is a concept easy to grasp.

From my perspective, if the all-encompassing notions of anti-leftist and America-first had not been adopted by the Trump supporters first, a name such as the Conservative Party would not be a good name for a party recruiting conservative Democrats, Libertarians, Constitutionals, Greens, and conservative Republicans. It would appear to be a face lift to the Republican Party.

The name John Doe Party cannot be argued against. It is the Party for America and regular Americans. It will draw anti-leftists and conservatives from the Republican Party for sure but it will also draw pro-Americans from the other parties, including the Democrats as more and more people are concerned for America.

For years Republicans had honestly espoused conservative values. They were the only "values" game in town. Perhaps they have been pretty good fakes over the years but for conservatives, there was no other Party that came close to being pro-American. Until the amnesty battle, and now the budget and the Obamacare battles, I thought conservatives and Republicans were on the same side ideologically. Now, I know better.

In mid-August 2013, Sean Hannity pulled no punches on his new disdain for the Republican Party:

*"This is it for me. Either they do everything they can do to stop Obamacare– or frankly, in my mind, it's time for a third party. This is now their moment of truth. We're going to learn who the real conservatives are. And we're going to learn who the real establishment people are. And then we're going to have to act accordingly".*

Ladies and gentlemen, the time has come and the new party is The John Doe Party.

It took a while but we now know who the establishment elites are. They run the Party behind closed doors and they are neither pro-American nor Republican. They are self-serving big money egotists. They feared Donald Trump from his first appearance on the scene because he has the wherewithal and the gumption to end their "party" with the Republican Party.

Now if only we little conservatives could get the smartest and most eloquent anti-leftist alive, Rush Limbaugh to finally give up the ghost on the GOP, I believe it would cause the floodgates to open and John Doe Americans would be leaving the Republican Party in droves with Chairman Limbaugh's permission and a little push. Yes, they would be heading for The John Doe Party.

Even Rush Limbaugh cannot hold out for long and, though he and Snerdley will not respond to anything I send them, I know that when Rush has had enough of the RINO Republican Party run by the elite establishment, Republicans elites will rue the day.

When Rush Limbaugh joins The John Doe Party and hopefully helps through his wisdom and resources to make the Party successful, he will help our movement more than Obama could ever think of helping the corrupt Democratic Party.

More and more conservatives are mad as hell! Like you and I, they believe that it is time to split the GOP into two separate political parties.

I predict that most former GOP will flock to The John Doe Party. Rush Limbaugh, Michael Savage, Sean Hannity, Glenn Beck, Sarah Palin and many others such as Michele Bachman, Michelle Malkin, Mark Steyn, Neil Bortz, Judge Andrew Napolitano, Laura Ingraham, and blasts from the past such as G. Gordon Liddy, who retired on July 27, 2012, would be in the on-deck circle of the new show: "The Break-Aways—a story of the flight from the RINO Republican Party." The Grand Old Party has been AWOL for some time now.

Some elitist spite-mongers that "hate the GOP to be put down though they deserve it," choose to say that the "right wing," of the Republican party, a derogatory term for conservatives, has decided to redefine the term "conservative." They say we should call ourselves the Conservative Party, and get it over with. Though I can appreciate their suggestions; they will not help our cause.

I like saying it so much let me do it again. We should call ourselves *The John Doe Party*, collect our gains and then rule America with Americans who think about America-first. Forget about the liberal progressive Democrats who want to pretend to be for the people. In the backs of their minds, they think of US, as "the proletariat."

The rest of the Republican Party are the "elite establishment." They should win the right to live with the new losing title, *The Republican Party*. We should never let them go ahead and join The John Doe Party to gain any sense of legitimacy for their RINO values.

There are many, many of us who are very saddened and disappointed in what has happened in the Republican Party. I have been a life-long Democrat, who most often voted Republican for conservative reasons. I would have voted for John F. Kennedy if I were old enough, and I did vote for Robert P. Casey Sr., both Democrats because they inspired Americans to be the best that we could be. They did not ask us to quit our jobs and see how great the government would be to us, as for years Barack Obama had secretly suggested.

Though anti-leftist nationalists can make laughing stocks out of the entire Republican Party, it would only be because Republicans have lost their moral compass. Yet, hurting Republicans is not something The

John Doe Party is inclined to want to do until we face them in a
National Election. Any Republican by values is better than any
Democrat by values.

If Republicans were staunch and true, and held on to their sense of the
founders' America, neither me, nor any of my conservative friends
would be predicting their demise. But, what is; is!

So, I am calling for the elite "establishment" (the Grand Old Party) to
check itself out on its new values. This group of RINOS needs to re-
unite and redefine the Republican Party as a group of patriots who
espouse American traditional values. I ask but I do think that this is
possible. Their leadership looks upon anti-leftists as the stubborn,
radical, intolerant, staunch religious right, of the far right wing of the
party of Lincoln. That can't work for me.

Elite Republicans are *fed up* and they resent the spewing of insults and
rhetoric toward the GOP. But, anti-leftists know the unkind rhetoric v
turncoat wimpy Republicans is well-deserved. The GOP
"establishment" deserves all the insults. Anti-leftists and conservatives
are doing a good job of separating the regular John Doe American half
of the pie from the liberal RINO progressive half, and the GOP, like it
or not is divided, though not yet separated. Separation will come when
the John Doe Party is taking registrants.

Anti-leftists do not like this type of negative speech coming from the left,
but it is even more disgusting when it comes from the elite in the
Republican Party.

## The John Doe Party is for Americans!

The John Doe party, as proposed in this book certainly has a much
better ring to it than "Know Nothings, "which was the one-time
pseudonym for the American Party in the mid 1800's. Moreover, the
term "John Doe Party" should be able to attract not only
disenfranchised conservative anti-leftist, ant-RINO Republicans but also
those Democrats, Greens, Libertarians, and Constitutionals who hold
strong pro-American views.

The new "John Doe Party" will replace the outmoded and cowardly Republican Party. In the residual Republican Party, the ghost of Burt Lahr should be cast to play the part of the Republican Party when the movie is finally made. He would make a great cowardly lion!

The John Doe Party is necessary as a party to embrace real Americans. Conservatives and other anti-leftists, such as those that are being disrespected and expelled from the Republican Party, as I speak will become the backbone of this patriotic American party—The John Doe Party.

Anti-leftists pro-Americans are happy to let both Republicans and Democrats swim in their own brine of corruption. Enjoy the political swamp. They have chosen a path that may help them but it does not help regular Americans. Let's hope all good dedicated Americans from each and every party join The John Doe Party in droves as it forms and as it embraces the values of Americanism.

# Chapter 13   John Doe Party & Elbert Lee Guillory Give Regular Americans Hope

## Hope Springs Eternal

Intrinsically each and every good American knows what being pro-American is all about. In a nutshell, it is for things that are good and it includes a sharp rejection of things that are bad. More technically, Americanism can be defined as a political or theological orientation advocating the preservation of the best in society and opposing radical changes to the American way of life. Another definition is the attachment or allegiance to the traditions, institutions, and ideals of the United States. They say that Americans in Europe have almost all preserved their Americanism.

It is clearly a puzzlement that the Republican Party has begun, piece by piece to replace its American foundation with the godless notion that the ends justify the means, and the only end for the Republican establishment today is to win elections. The people on the other hand see no value in a victory that provides the corrupt values of the Democratic Party. Why bother?

In his work, An Essay on Man, Alexander Pope offers consolation to those who continue to hope that something good will happen although it seems unlikely. In many ways, this fits the hopelessness that good Americans find today in the Republican Party, and for other reasons, across all of America.

*Hope springs eternal in the human breast;*
*Man never is, but always to be blessed:*
*The soul, uneasy and confined from home,*
*Rests and expatiates in a life to come.*

There are a number of interpretations of this classic poem but all have the same overall meaning. In the original poem shown above, Pope makes the argument that God did not give any of us knowledge of our future for it would be too heavy for us to bear. Instead, he gave us, in our ignorance, hope and optimism that the future will be good.

And, so, people throughout history continue to hope even though they have evidence that things more than likely will not turn out the way they want. We anti-leftists and conservatives, aka regular Americans, can use this as a rallying cry for the Republican Party, hoping it will change in a miraculous way. Yet, we come here in this book knowing that it has not happened yet and so we have a better hope for a great John Doe Party to replace it in our hearts.

As an alternate thought, as we have discussed in this book from Chapter One, there is always the hope that The John Doe Party will take the place of the Republican Party in our hearts and minds and that it will become a huge success for the nation. Hope Springs Eternal is often said during times of hardship and is meant to encourage people to keep hope alive.

Let us keep our hope alive in one of the two positive outcomes as defined. However, we do not have all day to decide which path to follow.

I observed the biggest snippet of hope in recent times. It came for me as I saw solid Democrats, whom I knew for decades, switching parties to be able to vote for Donald Trump in the 2016 Primary Election. The biggest chunk of hope came when Donald Trump was elected our 45th president. Now that hope is springing eternal.

Ironically, as Democrats may be seeing a spark of light in the promise of Donald Trump, I see elite Republicans beginning to hold on to Democratic values and Democratic notions instead of doing what they can to stop the threat brought forth by Democrat principles and the lack thereof.

Anti-leftist conservatives had been counting on Republicans to help America for years. It seemed natural. Since the Republican leadership turned its back on conservatives, I have been compelled to think this through for a root cause and a solution. I decided to write this book to help conservatives and anti-leftists have hope and a very good alternative to the new Republican way. Hope may spring eternal that Republicans will see the light but as in the poem, it is not likely. The John Doe Party, on the other hand has a great movie, Meet John Doe, as a great motivation tool. All the John Does together can beat the bad guys.

And so, we must create our own hope by knowing that we can build The John Doe Party as a better replacement for the Republican Party than the one-time Party of Lincoln ever hoped to be. We can begin as the Party of Trump in his second term (2020). When The John Doe Party blooms, we will all gain from fallout from Republicans, Democrats, Libertarians, Constitutionals, and Greens. There is even hope that Independents will find the John Doe Party suiting their ideals and a number will more than likely join the John Doe Party to help it along.

While we work to move Republicans to the John Doe Party, it is a good maxim to not besmirch the Republican Party as there are those who can gain immensely by giving up progressivism and moving to the values espoused by Republicans. Elbert Lee Guillory tells his story so we all know the power of moving towards the goodness in life.

## Elbert Lee Guillory

Hope comes from many sources. One of the greatest moments of hope for the country came forth just a few years ago as Louisiana State Senator Elbert Guillory (R-Opelousas) switched from the Democrat Party to the Republican Party. In his essay, he explains in detail why he made the decision to switch.

Along the way, he talks about the history of the Republican Party, from when it was founded as an abolitionist movement in 1854. The Senator then talks about how the welfare state is only a mechanism for politicians to control the black community. His succinct and pithy essay is very compelling and it is presented in its entirety below.

Since Elbert Guillory is a black man, his perspectives are quite salient. Unfortunately, like all black anti-leftist conservatives, Guillory will soon find himself being impugned and besmirched by his former party as if he has somehow gone mad.

Dr. Ben Carson, the great Pediatric Neuro-Surgeon from John Hopkins who gained additional fame when he spoke his piece at the National Prayer Breakfast, and then ran as a Presidential hopeful in the 2016 Republican Primary, and now is the highly-qualified head of the US Department of Housing and Urban Development (HUD), is an example of what will happen to the Senator. Carson is already being called 'token,' 'Uncle Tom,' 'Oreo,' and of course "Nigger."

Carson is not about to cave to such attacks and I have a good feeling about Guillory. He'll never cave either. What is right and good is right and good. Here is the essay he wrote about why he switched parties. It makes any good anti-leftist conservative melt-away and be recharged with hope. I love this essay:

"Hello, my name is Elbert Lee Guillory, and I'm the senator for the twenty-fourth district right here in beautiful Louisiana. Recently I made what many are referring to as a bold decision to switch my party affiliation to the Republican Party. I wanted to take a moment to explain why I became a Republican, and also to explain why I don't think it was a bold decision at all. It is the right decision not only for me but for all my brothers and sisters in the black community.

You see, in recent history the Democrat Party has created the illusion that their agenda and their policies are what's best for black people. Somehow it has been forgotten that the Republican Party was founded in 1854 as an abolitionist movement with one simple creed: that slavery is a violation of the rights of man.

Frederick Douglass called Republicans the Party of freedom and progress, and the first Republican president was Abraham Lincoln, the author of the Emancipation Proclamation. It was the Republicans in Congress who authored the thirteenth, fourteenth, and fifteenth amendments giving former slaves citizenship, voting rights, and due process of law.

The Democrats on the other hand were the Party of Jim Crow. It was Democrats who defended the rights of slave owners. It was the Republican President Dwight Eisenhower who championed the Civil Rights Act of 1957, but it was Democrats in the Senate who filibustered the bill.

You see, at the heart of liberalism is the idea that only a great and powerful big government can be the benefactor of social justice for all Americans. But the left is only concerned with one thing—control. And they disguise this control as charity. Programs such as welfare, food stamps—these programs aren't designed to lift black Americans out of poverty, they were always intended as a mechanism for politicians to control the black community.

The idea that blacks, or anyone for that matter, need the government to get ahead in life is despicable. And even more important, this idea is a failure. Our communities are just as poor as they've always been. Our schools continue to fail children. Our prisons are filled with young black men who should be at home being fathers. Our self-initiative and our self-reliance have been sacrificed in exchange for allegiance to our overseers who control us by making us dependent on them.

Sometimes I wonder if the word freedom is tossed around so frequently in our society that it has become a cliché.

The idea of freedom is complex and it is all-encompassing. It's the idea that the economy must remain free of government persuasion. It's the idea that the press must operate without government intrusion. And it's the idea that the emails and phone records of Americans should remain free from government search and seizure. It's the idea that parents must be the decision makers in regards to their children's education not some government bureaucrat.

But most importantly, it is the idea that the individual must be free to pursue his or her own happiness free from government dependence and free from government control. Because to be truly free is to be reliant on no one other than the author of our destiny. These are the ideas at the core of the Republican Party, and it is why I am a Republican.

So, my brothers and sisters of the American community, please join with me today in abandoning the government plantation and the Party of disappointment. So that we may all echo the words of one Republican leader who famously said, free at last, free at last, thank God Almighty, we are free at last..."

-- End of Guillory remarks –

Yes, the Republican Party is a much better choice than the Democrat Party, even though it is not holding 100% true to its own values.

The John Doe Party will take all of those values and add even more to help Americans be successful and to help Americans remain free for all time.

We cannot just think about it. It is time for positive action to bring about a positive result.

# LETS GO PUBLISH! Books by Brian Kelly:
(Sold at Amazon.com, and Kindle.).

Great Moments in Florida Gators Football. UF Football fron the start to today.

PATERNO: The Dark Days After Win # 409. Sky began to fall within days of win # 409 .

JoePa 409 Victories: Say No More!: Winningest Division I-A football coach ever

American College Football: The Beginning From before day one football was played.

Great Coaches in Alabama Football Challenging the coaches of every other program!

Great Coaches in Penn State Football the Best Coaches in PSU's football program

Great Players in Penn State Football The best players in PSU's football program

Great Players in Notre Dame Football The best players in ND's football program

Great Coaches in Notre Dame Football The best coaches in any football program

President Donald J. Trump, Master Builder: Solving the Student Debt Crisis!

President Donald J. Trump, Master Builder: It's Time for Seniors to Get a Break!

President Donald J. Trump, Master Builder: Healthcare & Welfare Accountability

President Donald J. Trump, Master Builder: "Make America Great Again"

President Donald J. Trump, Master Builder: The Annual Guest Plan

Great Players in Alabama Football from Quarterbacks to offensive Linemen Greats!

Great Moments in Alabama Football AU Football from the start. This is the book.

Great Moments in Penn State Football PSU Football, start--games, coaches, players,

Great Moments in Notre Dame Football ND Football, start, games, coaches, players

Four Dollars & Sixty-Two Cents—A Christmas Story That Will Warm Your Heart!

My Red Hat Keeps Me on The Ground. Darraggh's Red Hat is magical

Seniors, Social Security & the Minimum Wage. Things seniors need to know.

How to Write Your First Book and Publish It with CreateSpace

The US Immigration Fix--It's all in here.  Finally, an answer.

I had a Dream IBM Could be #1 Again  The title is self-explanatory

WineDiets.Com Presents The Wine Diet Learn how to lose weight while having fun.

Wilkes-Barre, PA; Return to Glory Wilkes-Barre City's return to glory

Geoffrey Parsons' Epoch... The Land of Fair Play Better than the original.

The Bill of Rights 4 Dummmies! This is the best book to learn about your rights.

Sol Bloom's Epoch ...Story of the Constitution The best book to learn the Constitution

America 4 Dummmies!  All Americans should read to learn about this great country.

The Electoral College 4 Dummmies! How does it really work?

The All-Everything Machine Story about IBM's finest computer server.

Brian has written 115 books. Others can be found at amazon.com/author/brianwkelly